PHILOSOPHY HACKS

HACKS

100 clever ways to help you understand and remember the most important theories

ROBERT ARP & MARTIN COHEN

CASSELL
ILLUSTRATED

An Hachette UK Company
www.hachette.co.uk

First published in Great Britain in 2018 by Cassell, an imprint of
Octopus Publishing Group Ltd, Carmelite House, 50 Victoria Embankment,
London EC4Y 0DZ
www.octopusbooks.co.uk
www.octopusbooksusa.com

Distributed in the US by Hachette Book Group, 1290 Avenue of the Americas,
4th and 5th Floors, New York, NY 10104

Distributed in Canada by Canadian Manda Group, 664 Annette St, Toronto,
Ontario, Canada M6S 2C8

ISBN 978-1-78840-039-8

A CIP catalogue record for this book is available from the British Library.

Printed and bound in China.

10 9 8 7 6 5 4 3 2 1

Hacks by Robert Arp: 1–5, 11–15, 18–20, 26–7, 29–30, 36–9, 44–7, 49–51, 56–61,
67–8, 72–4, 77, 80–4, 88, 91, 93, 98, 100

Hacks by Martin Cohen: 6–10, 16–17, 21–5, 28, 31–5, 40–3, 48, 52–5, 62–6, 69–71,
75–6, 78–9, 85–7, 89–90, 92, 94–7, 99

Commissioned by: Ellie Corbett
Senior Editor: Leanne Bryan
Junior Designer: Jack Storey
Design and layout: Simon Buchanan, Design 23
Illustrators: Design 23
Senior Production Manager: Peter Hunt
Picture Research Manager: Giulia Hetherington
Picture Library Manager: Jennifer Veall

Contents

Introduction

Distilling the essence

This is a book of shortcuts to philosophy. We all know the "long cuts" – the long and winding roads to big ideas offered by classic texts such as Kant's *Critique of Pure Reason*, Plato's *Dialogues* and Aristotle's *Logic*, to name just an iconic few. But, what if we don't actually have the time (or perhaps the inclination) to read these? Or what – now let's be radical for a moment – if you actually don't need to read them? Perhaps only a few ideas need to be brought out and examined? What if most of the millions of pages of philosophy, great and, well, not so great, are redundant, and within them there are just a few, relatively tiny, nuggets of insight? Although it may sound disgraceful to say this, philosophy is like that. You can read thousands of pages and only come across one or two ideas. And even then, the ideas are often poorly presented – perhaps because the philosopher was struggling to come to terms with his or her insight, or because the insight was only half worked out at the time.

More than almost any other subject, philosophy lends itself to a book such as this, a book in which thousands of years of thought, as well as thousands of pages of reflection, have been distilled to their barest of bare essentials, to a few hundred words, and even after this, to a one-paragraph "hack". Surely there is more to the big ideas of philosophy than can be summed up in so few words, and yet it doesn't do any harm to pinpoint a key aspect, to highlight the essential, to distil the essence. Furthermore, this book is not so much another mini-reference work summing up the history of the subject, but instead it is a much more unusual project – a word map with 100 firmly located landmarks. These landmarks are far from isolated, however. In the manner of a real tourist guide, we provide instructions on how to get to each of them, as well as guidelines on what to do when you get there.

Thinkers such as (above left to right) Mary Wollstonecraft, Jean-François Lyotard, Hannah Arendt and J. S. Mill have been considering big ideas for thousands of years.

The structure

The 100 philosophy hacks are arranged chronologically for no better reason than, well, they have to be arranged in some way. We recognize that philosophy is, after all, almost unique in its refusal to proceed steadily through time, gaining depth and wisdom. Instead, the Ancient thinkers continue to stand alongside their more recent followers as equals or, indeed, something better. Nonetheless, in as much as philosophy is a work-in-progress, it is sometimes useful to see how the ideas have evolved over time, and how debates have been shaped and reshaped over the centuries.

Each of the 100 philosophy hacks consists of three parts:

 1/ Helicopter view: This offers an overview of the philosophical idea, and usually its creator too, as well as a brief sketch of the context within which the insight was created.

 2/ Shortcut: This strips the idea down in order to expose and explain the core elements of the theory.

 3/ Hack: Short and to the point, this part offers a shortcut to making sense of the idea – and, crucially, remembering it.

So, that's the book. But where should you start? We suggest that you treat the book like a treat-box or bowl of potpourri. Just dip in anywhere you like and savour the ideas. But try not to consume too much in one sitting! These are big, deep ideas – and each one deserves to be chewed over a little.

Martin Cohen and Robert Arp

No.1
Hinduism's theism
God in all things

1/Helicopter view: Hinduism originated some 3,500 years ago around the Indus Valley in modern-day Pakistan. Unlike most other religions, Hinduism has no definite founder and no single creed. That said, there are some common core beliefs, one of which is the existence of an all-pervasive Supreme God that is both immanent (present throughout the universe) and transcendent (existing apart from the material universe). The qualities and forms of this God are represented by a multitude of deities – Brahma, the Creator; Vishnu, the Preserver; Shiva, the Destroyer; and many others – that emanate from such a being. This is perhaps Hinduism's primary paradox, since we are not sure if this God is "One in Supremacy" or "Many in Multitude", utterly unlike the universe or intimately intertwined with it. The Greek words μόνος (*monos*), πᾶς (*pás*) and θεός (*theós*) mean "one", "all" and "god", respectively, so monotheism is the belief in one god that is wholly distinct from the universe, while pantheism is the belief that god is identical to the universe, or the universe is a manifestation of God. In one of the central sacred Hindu texts, the *Bhagavad Gita* (see page 9), an avatar (incarnation) of the all-pervasive Supreme God called Krishna notes, "He who sees in me all things, and all things in me, is never far from me, and I am never far from him." This passage, and others like it, have led scholars to link Hinduism to pantheism.

2/Shortcut: In the *Bhagavad Gita*, Krishna also states, "All this world is pervaded by Me in My unmanifest aspect; all beings exist in Me, but I do not dwell in them." This passage suggests what we call *panentheism*, which means "god *in* all things". Pantheism makes God out to be too identified with the universe – it seems counterintuitive, for example, to say that God is equivalent to the workings and effects of the Black Plague or the machinations and horrors of the Holocaust. And monotheism generally places a huge wedge between God and the universe, making the Supreme Being appear to be an entity that is *radically distant* from the world. Thus, panentheism offers a happy medium of envisioning God in the universe, but not *of* the universe.

Late 12th to 13th-century bronzes from India representing Hinduism's Krishna, his consorts Rukmini and Satyabhama, and his mount Garuda (left).

See also //

2 Saṃsāra, p.8

3 Brahman, p.10

3/Hack: Monotheism has God too far removed from the universe, while pantheism equates God with the universe. It is argued that Hinduism offers a middle ground with panentheism, where God is seen as being *in* the universe, but not *of* the universe.

No.2
Saṃsāra Over and over again

1/Helicopter view: We sometimes want a second chance to do something, and we get it; and we nail it. At other times we get that second chance, then wish we had a third one! Imagine having to go through numerous lives to "get it right", so to speak, and being born into different bodies, possibly even different species. According to Hinduism, each of us has a soul (*atman*) that is trapped in a body and living one of many possible lives. At work in the universe around us are *dharma* and *karma*. Dharma refers to the harmonious order, unity and goodness present in the universe, while karma refers to the law of cause and effect by which each person can create his/her own destiny through thoughts, words and deeds. When a person's actions mirror dharma in that they bring about harmonious order, unity and goodness, they have created good consequences and might reap the rewards in this life, in a heavenly realm in which the atman is reborn for a period of time or in a future rebirth. On the other hand, when a person's actions are evil and vicious, then they have not aligned with dharma and will have to pay off their karmic debt in a process known as reincarnation, if not in this life, then in the next.

A bronze figure of a Kashmiri in meditation and a representation of the wheel of life (above).

2/ Shortcut: The process of reincarnation, or the evolution of the soul (atman) through many rebirths until all karmic debts have been settled, is called *saṃsāra*. In one of the central sacred Hindu texts, the *Bhagavad Gita* (see page 7), an avatar of the all-pervasive Supreme God called Krishna claims to be able to teach humanity the "actions and inactions" that will "lead them to be liberated from the evil of *saṃsāra*, the world of birth and death". Krishna goes on to note that the liberation from *saṃsāra* is *moksha*, which is an "absolute freedom" whereby one "has become Brahman, the divine itself". The kinds of attributes that help liberate a person from *saṃsāra* include being free from desire and anger; being self-controlled, self-aware and humble; recognizing that the universe is an illusion; and being concerned for the welfare of "all beings".

Detail from a representation of the wheel of life showing hell in all its graphic detail (below).

See also //
1 Hinduism's theism, p.6
3 Brahman, p.10

3/ Hack: *Saṃsāra* is the cosmic process of reincarnation endured by the soul (*atman*) until it reaches a state whereby, like the dharma present in the universe, it manifests harmonious order, unity and goodness.

No.3

Brahman
Source of all things

1/ Helicopter view: Humans have a natural need for an explanation for all the things they see, and interact with, in the universe. This is probably because we have a robust sense of consciousness compared with other animals, and we want to do more than simply exist. We want to flourish and better our existence. To do so requires an understanding of how things around us work, so that we can ultimately predict and control them. This desire to understand has led people to ask, "What's the explanation for the *entire universe itself*?" Thanks to the numerous sciences and methodologies that emerged as a result of the Scientific Revolution (see pages 94–5) of the 15th, 16th and 17th centuries, today's scientific answer to this question is the Big Bang, a theory that infers a cataclysmic birth of the universe from observing how that universe is expanding, cosmic background radiation, the abundance of the elements, and the laws of physics. However, if we wind the clock back 3,500 years or so, we find that the people of the Indus Valley, near the River Indus in modern-day Pakistan – who are known today as Hindus – were also trying to work out an explanation for the entire universe.

The Hindu god and supreme creator, Brahma (above left). In red, the figure for "Om", which is both a sacred sound and a spiritual icon.

10

2/Shortcut: Most Hindus venerate the existence of an all-pervasive Supreme God that is both immanent and transcendent, and whose qualities and forms are represented by a multitude of deities (Brahma, the Creator; Vishnu, the Preserver; Shiva, the Destroyer; and many others) that emanate from such a being. This all-pervasive Supreme God is behind the universe, and all the gods, as an Ultimate Reality. The Supreme God goes by different names, but is most commonly known as Brahman (not to be confused with Brahma, the Creator, or the priestly class of Brahmans). In some of the oldest of the sacred Hindu texts, the *Upanishads* (part of the *Vedas* from around the 7th century BCE), Brahman is described as "the One", as well as an "eternal, conscious, non-reducible, infinite, all-present, spiritual source of the finite and changing universe". Brahman is "in all things" and is the "source of all things".

See also //

1 Hinduism's theism, p.6

2 Saṃsāra, p.8

37 Ultimate cause of everything, p.78

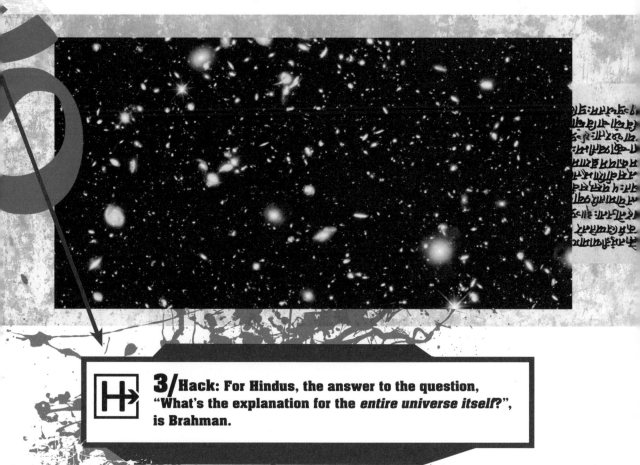

3/Hack: For Hindus, the answer to the question, "What's the explanation for the *entire universe itself*?", is Brahman.

No.4
Cosmic dualism
Love and hate in constant struggle

Zoroaster // c.628–551 BCE

1/Helicopter view: From the time of our earliest ancestors, humans have attributed benevolent as well as malevolent motivations not only to other humans, but also to animals, plants, features of the land, the weather and various other phenomena in the universe. Put simply, there are good entities that do good things and bad entities that do bad things. The Greek words κόσμος (*kósmos*) and δύο (*duo*) mean "ordered universe" and "two", respectively, so *cosmic dualism* is the belief that there are two fundamental types of principles at work in the universe: one that is good, life-giving, harmonious and just, and one that is bad, death-dealing, disharmonious and unjust. However, as humans, we need to give a face to powerful forces; we naturally anthropomorphize and humanize the world in order to help us make sense of things, to explain them, to understand them – or to know whom we should be thanking for our good fortune or begging for deliverance from our misfortunes.

The Faravahar icon (above) was a symbol of Zoroastrianism, the religion of the Persian Empire. It is also a common symbol of modern-day Iran.

2/Shortcut: Cosmic dualism has been associated with the Persian/Iranian mystic Zoroaster (*c.*628–551 BCE). He not only preached ideas about a formation of the universe, an eschatology (the belief in an "end of days"), a resurrection of the dead, a heaven and a hell that may have influenced Jewish theology – and, hence, Christianity and Islam – but also had a dream in which he saw the High Good God, Ahura Mazdā, with all his good minions battling the High Evil God, Angra Mainyu, with all his little imps in the early formation of the Earth. These two were not merely the personification of good and evil, truth and lie, right and wrong, they were *The Good* and *The Evil*, *The Truth* and *The Lie*, and *The Right* and *The Wrong*. And, because Zoroaster also had a robust concept of free will, except for the good and evil caused by humans, they were also the source of all these opposing phenomena in the universe. Ahura Mazdā and Angra Mainyu not only offered an ultimate explanation for all the naturally occurring positives and negatives experienced by humans, but could also act as models for human behaviour.

The High Evil God Angra Mainyu, represented here by a lion, is shown killing the primeval bull (below).

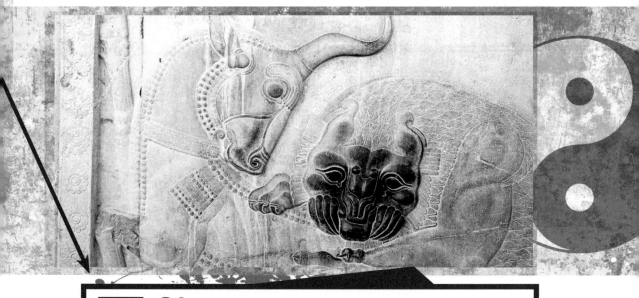

3/Hack: Zoroaster personified all things good, life-giving and harmonious in the High Good God, Ahura Mazdā, while Angra Mainyu was the personification of things evil, death-dealing and disharmonious.

No.5
The Golden Rule
Central to peace and prosperity

1/Helicopter view: Many would argue that Confucius (551–479 BCE) is the most influential thinker in the history of East Asian philosophy, and it is no exaggeration to say that his philosophy saturates Chinese culture to this day. Living and teaching during the turmoil of the Zhou Dynasty, Confucius tried defining ethical and political philosophies that would return China to the serene days of the Shang Dynasty. He argued that peace and tranquillity could only occur when people become virtuous, sufficiently self-controlled in their actions and reactions to situations so as to "hit the mark" between the "too much" and the "too little". In the *Analects*, a great collection of his teachings, Confucius notes, "Perfect is the virtue which is according to the Mean! Rare have they long been among the people, who could practise it!" According to Confucius, there are a number of virtues: self-control, respect for one's elders, respect for one's family, courage, generosity and friendliness, to name but a few. A central moral virtue for Confucius is 仁 (*ren*), which can be translated as "goodness", "correct action", "right conduct" or even "humanity". *Ren* is like your conscience or the "little voice in your head" that tells you what to do in a situation.

Confucius // 551–479 BCE

Confucius was the essence of the Chinese sage: a philosopher who presented himself merely as a transmitter of wisdom and who himself invented nothing.

2/ Shortcut: More than telling you what you *should do* in a given situation, *ren* also tells you what you *should not do*. This is the "other side of the coin", so to speak. The classic Golden Rule, as formulated in the Bible, in Matthew 7:12, goes like this: "Do unto others as you would have them do unto you." However, in the *Analects*, there is an exchange between Confucius and one of his pupils in which the pupil asks, "Is there any one word that could guide a person throughout life?" and Confucius replies, "How about 'reciprocity' – never impose on others what you would not impose on yourself." Scholars have called this wording the Silver Rule – it is a negative phrasing of the Golden Rule.

See also //

60 Immanuel Kant's moral theory, p.124

68 Good for the majority, p.140

3/ Hack: Confucius' Golden Rule has been described as a Silver Rule, given that it is phrased in the negative: never impose on others what you would not impose on yourself.

No.6
Taoism's yin and yang
The eternal cycle of creation

1/Helicopter view: "Yin" and "yang" are two eternally intertwined forces, two aspects of everything in reality. Yin, the feminine aspect, is dark, soft and yielding. Yang, the masculine aspect, is bright (light), hard and inflexible. Everything in the world consists of both elements, and everything is in a state of flux, changing to become more yin or more yang. The lesson is that we should strive to transcend the world of distinctions.

It is important not to make overly simple Western assumptions about the terminology – and, in particular, not to object that the "feminine" element, yin, is negative and passive, while the masculine element, yang, is positive and active. Because not only is such commentary misdirected, it completely obscures the core idea of the yin-yang interplay: in which yin becomes yang, and yang becomes yin in an eternal cycle of creation and destruction. The two forces are opposites, yes, but they are also the same; united by change, they merge into each other. It is change – not yin, not yang – that is the fundamental property of the universe.

Lao Tzu // 6th–5th century BCE

2/ Shortcut: The Chinese sage Lao Tzu (6th–5th century BCE) is credited with originally expounding the doctrine of yin and yang. He is counted in China as a contemporary of Confucius (551–479 BCE; see pages 14–15) and as one of the four great sages, along with Mo Tzu (5th–4th century BCE) and Chuang Tzu (4th century BCE). In the West, however, commentators dispute whether such a person ever existed, or whether he may instead be a kind of assemblage of various ancient, long-obscured thinkers and traditions. A similar dispute surrounds the classic book of Taoism, known as the *Tao Te Ching*, which is usually regarded as Lao Tzu's greatest work. The notion of yin and yang is just one of a number of enormously influential ideas that appears there. The following is our version (there are many interpretations) of some of the enigmatic aphorisms, juxtaposing yin and yang, which appear in a standard translation of the original text:

In the original text of the *Tao Te Ching*, the Chinese sage Lao Tzu (shown, below left, riding an ox) uses evocative comparisons to juxtapose the intertwined forces of "yin" and "yang".

See also //

1 Hinduism's theism, p.6
4 Cosmic dualism, p.12
37 Ultimate cause of everything, p.78

Human beings are born soft and flexible;
yet when they die are stiff and hard…

Plants sprout soft and delicate, yet when they
die they are withered and dry…

Thus the hard and stiff are disciples of death,
the soft and flexible are disciples of life.

Thus an inflexible army is not victorious,
an unbending tree will break.

The stiff and massive will be lessened;
the soft and fluid will increase.

3/ Hack: At the heart of the doctrine of yin and yang is the idea that all knowledge is relative. All judgements – not just moral or aesthetic ones – are rooted in context.

No.7
Jainism's *ahimsa*
Lives dedicated to doing no harm

1/ Helicopter view: Originating in around 500 BCE, Jainism is today a religion with perhaps five million followers, as well as an ancient philosophical school that offers *ahimsā* or "non-violence" as its central ethical principle. The term *ahimsā* translates as "cause no injury, do no harm". The name of the movement comes from the term for a spiritual conqueror, *Jina*, but this is a victory over illusions, and the reward is wisdom. All Jainist monks must take five solemn vows known as *vratas*, as outlined in their oldest surviving text, the *Acaranga Sutra*. These vows commit them to dedicate their lives to *ahimsā* ("non-violence"); *satya* ("truth"); *asteya* ("not stealing"); *brahmacharya* ("celibacy or chastity"); and *aparigraha* ("non-attachment").

The pledges are interpreted absolutely by Jainism's followers, so that the interdiction against violence precludes the killing of plants. Fortunately, you can eat still eat a plant's leaves, flowers, fruit and nuts, but the plant itself must be left to flourish. It also means that Jainists try to avoid treading on ants and swallowing microbes! Curiously, suicide is permitted – but only by means of starvation and exposure. Although a call for non-violence also features prominently in Hindu and Buddhist canonical texts, no one takes it more seriously than the Jainists.

2/Shortcut: Jainism has something in common with the concept of yin and yang (see pages 16–17) in that everything is seen as being interconnected and relative. There is no god, but rather the universe is the collective consciousness of all things. This, of course, feeds into the interdiction against violence. So, too, does the idea that everything has an infinite number of aspects – it all depends on how it is viewed. Everything is the same and yet, equally, everything is different. Jainism seeks a very particular kind of spiritual victory for its followers: that of triumphing over life's otherwise perpetual stream of rebirths through an ethical and spiritual life.

A hand with a wheel on the palm (below right) symbolizes *ahiṃsā* in Jainism. The "Om" symbol (below left) is often used to signify the famous mantra.

See also //

1 Hinduism's theism, p.6
3 Brahman, p.10

3/Hack: For Jainists, all living beings possess the spark of the divine spiritual energy; therefore, to hurt another being is to hurt oneself.

No.8
Buddhism's *dukkha*
Looking on the dark side

 1/Helicopter view: Siddhartha Gautama, the historical Buddha (born 563 BCE), once summarized his own teachings in this way: "It is only *dukkha* that I describe, and the cessation of *dukkha*." For his followers, no single word in the English language can adequately capture the full depth, range and subtlety of the concept of *dukkha*. Over the years, many translations have been used, of which "suffering" is only the most common. Each term is said to convey different aspects, and Buddhism itself emphasizes the need to continually broaden and deepen one's understanding.

In *An Introduction to Buddhism: Teachings, History and Practices*, one translator in the English language, Peter Harvey, tried to express the concept of *dukkha* as follows: "Birth is *dukkha*, aging is *dukkha*, sickness is *dukkha*, death is *dukkha*; sorrow, lamentation, pain, grief and despair are *dukkha*; association with what one dislikes is *dukkha*, separation from what one likes is *dukkha*, not to get what one wants is *dukkha*..." Long as this list may be, it hardly touches upon the desirability, within Buddhist philosophy, of transcendence – of transcending dukkha and becoming...indifferent.

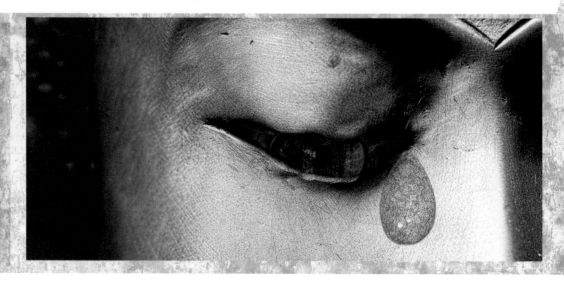

2/Shortcut: The original word, *dukkha*, is Pali, which is a variation of Sanskrit, the language of ancient and medieval India. It can mean a lot of things – even, perhaps surprisingly, "happiness". This is because happiness is always temporary, and will eventually bring its opposite. For Buddhists, happiness is also a state that must be transcended.

Buddhists advise enquirers to simply use the word *dukkha* in the hope that they will discover its real meaning over time. Nonetheless, some understanding of *dukkha* is critical to a grasp of Buddhism's Four Noble Truths. These are similarly obscure, but sometimes rendered as: the truth of suffering; the truth of the origin of suffering; the truth of the cessation of suffering; and the truth of the path to the cessation of suffering.

Buddhist art flourished and evolved along with Hindu and Jain art, with Buddhist temples hosting striking images, such as this Stupa drum panel (below) showing Buddha's conception.

See also //
9 Buddhism's *anicca*, p.22
10 Buddhism's *nirvāna*, p.24

3/Hack: Buddhism's *dukkha* (or "suffering") sounds pretty grim because, well, it is. And, for Buddhists, the worst thing about life is that it's not even possible to look forward to the end of *dukkha* because we are eternally reincarnated – usually as something even worse! That's *dukkha*!

No.9
Buddhism's *anicca*
The fleeting nature of all things

1/ Helicopter view: In Buddhism (*c*.450 BCE), "impermanence" (from the Pali word, *anicca*) is one of the three "marks", or fundamental characteristics, of the physical universe, the other two being *dukkha* or "suffering" (see pages 20–1) and *anatta* or "insubstantiality" (see page 25). In order to "see things as they really are", it is necessary to consistently interpret the world in the light of these three characteristics. In contrast, ignorance of these three characteristics, or self-deception about them, is the cause of much human misery. Such ignorance, by creating false hopes and unrealistic desires and aims in life, becomes a net in which the individual is caught. A lack of awareness or a distortion of these three basic facts of existence can only lead to frustration, disappointment and despair.

The early 20th-century Buddhist preacher Piyadassi Maha Thera (1914–1998) described *anicca* in the following way: "We cannot say of anything, animate or inanimate, organic or inorganic, 'this is lasting'; for even while we are saying this, it would be undergoing change. All is fleeting; the beauty of flowers, the bird's melody, the bee's hum and a sunset's glory."

Buddhist funerals are not entirely sad occasions, as Buddhists believe that death is only part of a cycle of rebirth and a reminder of the Buddhist teachings of impermanence.

2/Shortcut: In Buddhism, the three fundamental characteristics of the physical universe are impermanence, suffering and insubstantiality, with impermanence and insubstantiality applying to both living and inanimate things, while suffering is something that can only be experienced by conscious beings. The inanimate, however, can be, and very often is, a cause of woe for living beings – for example, floods may lead to damage to property and hardship, and thus cause mental anguish. In that sense, all three factors apply to everything.

For Buddhists, insight and wisdom consist of, and come from, the experience and recognition of the working of the three characteristics on one's own body and self. The path to such enlightenment starts with an appreciation of the impermanence of all things. The *Maha-Parinibbana Sutta*, a revered Buddhist text, says:

See also //

8 Buddhism's *dukkha*, p.20
10 Buddhism's *nirvāna*, p.24

"Impermanent are all component things,
They arise and cease, that is their nature:
They come into being and pass away,
Release from them is bliss supreme."

Even today, at Buddhist funerals held within the most traditional cultures, this verse is recited by monks to remind the mourners of the transient and evanescent nature of life.

3/Hack: Change, or impermanence, is the essential characteristic of everything in the universe.

No.10
Buddhism's *nirvāna*
The elusive destination sought by the wise

1/ Helicopter view: In Buddhism (c.450 BCE), *nirvāna* (or "liberation") is the goal at the end of the spiritual path and is summed up in the release of the soul from the cycle of rebirth. The literal meaning of the Sanskrit word *nirvāna* is "blown out" and is conveyed in two examples given in the foundation texts. In one, husks of corn are imagined being blown away, leaving the grain, and in another, metaphorical flames of desire are extinguished or blown out.

Busts of a group of serene Buddhists whose expressions hint at the bliss to be found in approaching *nirvāna*.

In the language of Buddhist philosophy, *nirvāna* marks the "cessation of *dukkha*" (see page 20) – in the sense of striving or, as it is often put, "suffering" – and the extinction of the "three fires", namely, passion, hatred and ignorance. It is a state sought by many, but only attainable by very few. One Buddhist sutra describes the attributes of the Blessed One thus: "Serene and inspiring, confident, calming, his senses at peace, his mind at peace, having attained the utmost tranquillity and poise, tamed, guarded, his senses restrained."

Also, words attributed to Buddha, while in conversation with Chunda, the Blacksmith, indicate some of the necessary steps on the path: "He who gives away shall have real gain. He who subdues himself shall be free; he shall cease to be a slave of passions. The righteous man casts off evil, and by rooting out lust, bitterness and illusion do we reach *nirvāna*."

2/Shortcut: *Nirvāna* is often described within Buddhism as the state of *anatta*, meaning "non-self" or "becoming substance-less" (see page 22), and *sunyata* ("emptiness"). However, this is only because, as one contemporary American academic, Omar Edward Moad (from Qatar University), has put it, *nirvāna* can only be explained to the "unenlightened" by negation. An example of this is a simile used by the Buddha in his dialogue with a disciple called Vacchagotama. Buddha asks whether a fire, when it is extinguished, can be said to have gone north, south, east or west. Of course, the obvious answer is that the fire no longer exists. In fact, *nirvāna* is really more about "realization" than "non-existence". As another Buddhist disciple, Nagasena, explains, only "a mind that is purified, lofty, straight and without obstructions, without temporal desires, sees *nirvāna*".

Buddhists believe that it is a misunderstanding of their philosophy to equate *nirvāna* with non-existence. They complain that Western philosophers such as Friedrich Nietzsche (1844–1900; see pages 148–9) and Arthur Schopenhauer (1788–1860; see pages 134–5) failed to understand, let alone communicate, the system fully because they did not adopt Buddhist practices aimed at enlightenment.

See also //
8 Buddhism's *dukkha*, p.20
9 Buddhism's *anicca*, p.22

 3/Hack: Within Buddhism, *nirvāna* is the term for the absolute unity to which all things, not just human souls, ultimately aspire.

Water, water everywhere...
Search for the source

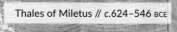

Thales of Miletus // c.624–546 BCE

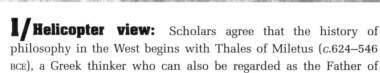

1/Helicopter view: Scholars agree that the history of philosophy in the West begins with Thales of Miletus (*c*.624–546 BCE), a Greek thinker who can also be regarded as the Father of Science in the West. While Greek mythologists around him were using stories to explain various phenomena – What causes the Sun to move across the sky? A god. What makes it rain? A god – Thales attempted to explain natural objects and phenomena using hypotheses, arguments and evidence. Also, by virtue of the fact that he was trying to *convince* or *persuade* people using natural explanations – as opposed to supernatural or mythological ones – he was putting forward arguments in the realm of logic, which is now recognized as the bedrock discipline of philosophy. Two main anecdotes are used to demonstrate Thales's scientific prowess. The first is that, according to *The Histories* of Herodotus (*c*.484–420 BCE), as well as several other philosophers, Thales predicted the solar eclipse of 28 May 585 BCE. This prediction would have required astronomical observations combined with mathematical calculations. The second is that he predicted an excellent olive-growing season one year and bought up all the olive presses in the Greek cities of Miletus and Chios, so he could profit by renting them out to meet the increase in demand. This prediction would have required agricultural and other natural observations. Thales used this last venture to demonstrate the practicality of his way of thinking to all those who used to tease him for "wasting his time" with his pursuits.

After predicting a good olive season Thales is said to have bought up all the olive presses (like this traditional example, right) in Miletus and Chios, so that he could profit from an increased demand for pressing.

2/Shortcut: As well as trying to find natural and scientific explanations for objects and events, Thales went further in searching for a single, unifying "thing", which he believed underlay everything in existence. When he looked around, he noticed that everything seemed to require water in some form to move, work, act or even exist. Indeed, you might place a seed in the soil, but nothing will happen until you water it. Any living thing seems to die without water. Water is in the ground, in the air as clouds and mist, and appears as dew and sweat. Aristotle (384–322 BCE; see pages 46–53) would later note that Thales's ἀρχή (*arche*), his "beginning", "origin", "principle" or "source of action/motion" of nature, was a single material substance, namely, water.

See also //
37 Ultimate cause of everything, p.78
39 The Uncaused Cause, p.82

3/Hack: The history of philosophy in the West begins with Thales of Miletus, who believed that a single, unifying "thing" underlies everything in existence. This is a single material substance: water.

No.12
Never stepping in the same river twice
We are and we are not

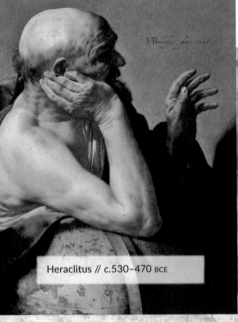

Heraclitus // c.530–470 BCE

 1/ Helicopter view: Things seem to move and change around us constantly. At a macro level, we're told that the universe is expanding, while at a micro level, we're told that subatomic particles are constantly "vibrating" and "waving". The Greek philosopher Parmenides of Elea (*c.*500 BCE; see page 30) argued that change and movement are but illusions, and are, in fact, impossible. He used logic and reasoning to come to this conclusion. For something to change, say a cat moving off a mat, means it has to go from being to non-being: the "being" of the cat on the mat to the "non-being" of the cat off the mat, and vice versa. But, argues Parmenides, even non-being is being by virtue of the fact that we can think and talk about it, so there really is no such thing as non-being. Thus, there is no such thing as change – it's all an illusion! "All is", as Parmenides tells us. Now imagine taking the completely opposite position and believing that permanence, stability or rest are the things that are illusions.

Plato's familiarity with the Heraclitean theory that all sensible things are "forever flowing" contributed to his doubt that we can ever know the sensible world, and hence to his Theory of Forms.

2/Shortcut: In contrast to Parmenides of Elea, who believed that there is no such thing as change, Heraclitus of Ephesus (*c.*530–470 BCE) thought the opposite to be true. You may have heard his famous dictum, "You can't step in the same river twice", which was apparently misquoted by the Greek philosopher Plato (428–348 BCE; see pages 40–5) in his dialogue *Cratylus* (see page 32). What Heraclitus actually wrote was "Στον ίδιο ποταμό και οι δύο βήμα και δεν βήμα, είμαστε και δεν είναι", which translates as, "In the same river we both step and do not step; we are and are not." Heraclitus believed the universe to be in a constant state of flux. Hence, in the same way that when you step from the bank into the body of a river you have always known, and the waters flowing over your feet will never be the same waters that flowed even a moment before, so, too, when you "step into the world" that you think you know, where you think things are stable, in reality they are not. They're constantly moving, adjusting, changing, morphing, altering, and going from being to non-being to both being and non-being at the same time. So, whereas Parmenides thinks that "All is", Heraclitus believes "All is and is not" (at the same time).

See also //

13 An impossible runner's feat, p.30

14 Finger wagging to make a point, p.32

3/Hack: Heraclitus thought that when you "step into the world" that you think you know, where you think things are stable, they are not in reality because everything is constantly in flux.

No.13
An impossible runner's feat

The illusion of change and motion

Zeno // 490–430 BCE

1/ Helicopter view: Let's say I believe in a God, whom I define as being *All-Powerful*. Now I ask the following question: "Can this All-Powerful God create a boulder that cannot be destroyed?" I have just generated what is known as a *paradox*. A paradox is a claim or set of claims that seem(s) contradictory or absurd, but may nonetheless be non-contradictory, rational, consistent and/or true. Paradoxes are important logical tests: they help us think through problems of vagueness and ambiguity in our language (for example: What do we really mean by *God*?); they force us to resolve the issue by "taking a position" and to think critically by providing an argument for our position (how you "solved" the paradox). One of the first thinkers to utilize paradoxes to make people think was Zeno of Elea (*c.*490–430 BCE). He was a student of Parmenides of Elea (*c.*500 BCE; see page 28), and put together several paradoxes to support Parmenides' doctrine that, contrary to the evidence of one's senses, change and motion are illusions. Zeno actually put together ten paradoxes, but the one that's most frequently discussed involves a runner on a racetrack.

The problem of infinity reoccurs throughout Zeno's famous paradoxes, raising fundamental issues for mathematics, astronomy and physics, not just for runners.

2/Shortcut: In his Runner's Paradox, Zeno asks us to imagine Achilles, the great warrior of Homer's *Iliad*, in a race trying to reach a goal on a straight racetrack. In order to reach the goal, Achilles must first run half the distance, but to do that, he must run half of *that* distance, and so on. So, if Achilles started at the zero of a 10-m (32-ft) long racetrack, before he could reach the 10-m (32-ft) mark, he would need to reach the 5-m (16-ft) mark, but before he could reach the 5-m (16-ft) mark, he would need to reach the 2.5-m (8-ft) mark and so on, ad infinitum. Thus, reasoned Zeno, Achilles can never actually run anywhere because it requires him to complete an infinite number of tasks, which is impossible! Through the centuries, many solutions to this paradox have been suggested. Some have argued that if we simply add up all the distances, then Achilles could do it. However, others have countered that it's not possible to add up the infinite.

See also //

12 Never stepping in the same river twice, p.28

14 Finger wagging to make a point, p.32

3/Hack: Zeno's Runner's Paradox states that finishing a race is impossible because to finish, a runner must first run half the track, and to run half the track, he/she must run a quarter of the track, and so on, creating an infinite, and therefore impossible, number of tasks.

No.14
Finger wagging to make a point Words fail

1/ Helicopter view: A fundamental way in which we use language is to categorize the world around us. In philosophical terminology, we might say that when we use language to name things with words, we delimit the realm of being, enabling us to refer confidently to one part of reality rather than another. Consider basic biological classification, which we learn as children: A is for aardvark, B is for bear, C is for cat, and so on. The Greek philosopher Plato (428–348 BCE; see pages 40–5) considers the nature of language and its relationship to naming things in reality in his dialogue *Cratylus* (see page 29). Given that Socrates (470–399 BCE; see pages 38–9) was Plato's teacher, most of Plato's dialogues feature Socrates in discussion with at least one interlocutor about a particular topic. *Cratylus* presents Socrates in discussion with Cratylus (mid–late 5th century BCE) and Hermogenes (5th–4th century BCE) about naming things, with the question of whether things "naturally" lend themselves to "name-ability" and we accept this after the fact or, alternatively, if it is the case that people control naming conventions and agree to name things upfront. Cratylus ultimately offers an interesting set of arguments in that dialogue. However, it is how he is characterized by Plato's student Aristotle (384–322 BCE; see pages 46–53) that is much more intriguing for history *and* philosophy books.

The meaning of a word like "apple" evolves and changes depending on its uses and significations.

2/Shortcut: Whereas Zeno took Parmenides of Elea's arguments to their logically extreme conclusion, it seems that Cratylus took Heraclitus' arguments about the world being constantly in a state of flux to their logically extreme conclusion. According to Aristotle in his *Metaphysics*, Cratylus thought that since everything in the universe is constantly changing, nothing is able to stay still long enough for a person to "get a grasp of it". So, if nothing can be grasped fully, then "nothing could truly be affirmed". In fact, things are changing so constantly and so *quickly* that once a word is uttered about something, that thing has already changed and what was said about it is no longer true. Thus, thought Cratylus, the best thing to do is to keep your mouth closed and respond to people by wagging your finger!

See also //

12 Never stepping in the same river twice, p.28

13 An impossible runner's feat, p.30

3/Hack: According to Cratylus, things change so quickly that, as soon as a word is uttered about something, it immediately becomes false. For this reason, it is always best to remain quiet and respond to people by wagging your finger!

No.15
Striving for tyranny
Might makes right

1/ Helicopter view: Charles Darwin (1809–1882) gave us the theory of the "survival of the fittest", according to which the strongest of a species in an environment will live long enough to reproduce. In the animal kingdom, being dominant – in essence, being a bully – rather goes with the territory when you are the biggest, fastest or even cleverest of your kind. The alphas will always lay claim to food and meet their other basic needs first. Humans are no different, as can be witnessed early on in the school environment. When little Sallys and Johnnys grow up, they often retain that oppressive, animalistic characteristic, and – if they get enough power and control in a social setting – can allow it to run amok. The following is perhaps an overused example, but it still hits the message home: consider the Third Reich in Nazi Germany in around 1940. The Nazis were in power, and a lot of the German populace was either complicit with, went along with or did nothing to prevent Nazi policies because, well, they were the laws of the land! Because the Nazis had declared themselves to be better than everyone else in the world, and had written policies, procedures and laws to reflect that assessment, this became fact, the truth, what was good and what was right.

Hitler salutes a parade of his Nazi SA troops in Nuremberg in 1935 (right). Only two years after gaining power in Germany, he had become almost an idol of the people.

2/Shortcut: The concept of a dominant individual or group being superior can be boiled down to the phrase, "Might makes right." Another memorable formulation is this: "The Golden Rule – he/she who has the gold makes all the rules." One of the first thinkers in the history of Western philosophy to put forward a set of arguments in favour of this position was Thrasymachus (*c*.459–400 BCE) in Book I of the *Republic*, by the Greek philosopher Plato (428–348 BCE; see pages 40–5). There, another Greek philosopher Socrates (470–399 BCE; see pages 38–9) argues with Thrasymachus that one should be just, while Thrasymachus argues that one should be unjust so as to become a tyrant, which is the goal of political life. Thrasymachus is pushing for one to become the ideal bully in life. After all, if you have all the power, you can make all the rules – you can actually *create* what is right and what is wrong.

See also //
19 The Republic, p.42
23 Aristotle's happiness, p.50
44 Machiavelli's Prince, p.92

 3/Hack: Thrasymachus argues that becoming a tyrant is the goal of political life. If you have all the power, you can make all the rules – in short, "Might makes right."

No.16
Aesara of Lucania's tripartite soul
Reclaiming a place for desire

1/Helicopter view: The idea that the soul — or as we might say today, the human psyche — can usefully be divided into three parts is usually associated with the Greek philosopher Plato (428–348 BCE; see pages 40–5). What is not usually remembered is that Plato essentially popularized other people's ideas, and, in this case, the concept of the division of the soul seems to have originated with the Pythagorean philosopher Aesara of Lucania (c.4th or 3rd century BCE). It is thought that Aesara was one of the daughters of the Greek philosopher and mathematician Pythagoras (c.570–490 BCE), but it is more likely that she was simply a respected follower. In the only known fragment of her writings, Aesara specifically describes the parts and powers of the soul, as well as arguing that there is a parallel between the health and balance of the individual psyche and the correct management of society — the equation at the heart of Plato's most famous work, *Republic* (see pages 42–3).

Pythagoreans offer a hymn to the rising sun in Fyodor Bronnikov's painting of 1869.

2/Shortcut: Aesara describes a three-part division of the soul, made up of:

(1) The element of mind, providing the ability to make judgements and to think;

(2) The element of spirit, providing courage and strength; and

(3) The element of desire, which enables love and friendliness.

See also //

28 Plotinus' three hypostases, p.60

51 René Descartes' substance dualism, p.106

In Plato's later division of the soul, which was repeated by the Greek philosopher Aristotle (384–322 BCE; see pages 46–53), the three-parts division of the soul become *nous* (the "rational"), *thumosis* (the "spirited") and *epithumia* (the "appetitive"). Aesara's view of desire seems more positive than that of either Plato or Aristotle, and her view of happiness is certainly broader and not as intellectual.

The concept of the tripartite soul is so important to Plato that it appears in no less than three of his dialogues, notably his *Phaedo*, *Phaedrus* and *Republic*. In the last of these, *Republic*, Plato develops the argument that the three drivers of behaviour also provide a better understanding of human societies, with each aspect essentially corresponding to an economic stratum of society.

In more psychological terms, however, each part of the psyche is believed to have its own motivations and desires: the reasoning part is motivated to seek truth and knowledge; the appetitive part seeks food, drink, material wealth and sex; and, lastly, the spirited part seeks glory, and is driven by a need for honour and recognition.

3/Hack: Aesara of Lucania stresses the need for the unity of the soul. Unlike later philosophers, she grants pleasure a positive role and recognizes the part it plays in the good life.

No.17
Socratic ignorance
A different kind of wisdom

Plato // 428–348 BCE

Socrates // 470–399 BCE

1/ Helicopter view: The saying, "The only thing I know is that I know nothing" is widely attributed to Socrates in Plato's dialogues, but it actually occurs nowhere in this form in the works of Plato (428–348 BCE; see pages 40–5). In fact, the nearest Socrates (470–399 BCE) comes to declaring his ignorance is when, in Plato's *Apology*, he says that, having talked with many people who thought they knew about more things than they really did, he was at least wiser than them since he didn't assume he knew things that he did not, in fact, know. In short, Socrates was aware of his own ignorance.

Marble statues of the Greek philosophers Socrates and Plato flanking the main entrance to the Academy of Athens. Socrates is seen in the classic thinker's pose.

2/ Shortcut: Socrates never professes ignorance regarding matters that he thinks are most important, namely ethical matters. For example, in a dialogue that supposedly takes place with Protagoras (c.490–420 BCE), who represents sophism – the clever use of words to win arguments rather than to find the truth – Socrates firmly defends the following points: (1) No one desires evil; (2) Nobody is wrong intentionally or knowingly; (3) Virtue is knowledge; and (4) Virtue is sufficient for happiness.

See also //
18 The Forms, p.40
20 Knowledge, p.44

And so, although the superficial view and the popular appeal of Socrates as a kind of radical sceptic have tended to dominate Western philosophy, more conscientious scholars note that Socrates is a very different kind of thinker. So what really underlies this notion of Socratic ignorance?

Sara Ahbel-Rappe, Professor of Classics at the University of Michigan, argues that the Platonic dialogues depict a Socrates with a profound commitment to self-knowledge through inner examination and self-inquiry. She suggests that these are tools for a contemplative practice that teaches us how to investigate the mind and its objects directly. Another contemporary thinker, Peter Hubral, goes even further and argues that Socrates is praising a kind of wisdom that is only obtainable through an Eastern meditative approach, which reawakens the esoteric knowledge that Plato calls *gnósis*. Hubral recalls that, far from knowing nothing, Plato has Socrates praising the process of *anámnesis*, which can be roughly translated as "recollection".

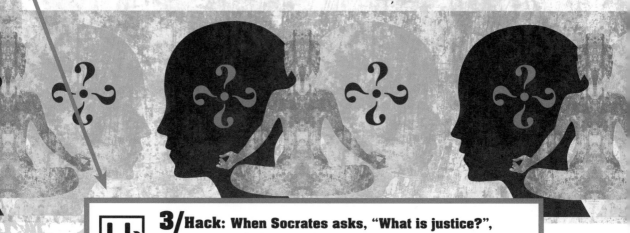

3/ Hack: When Socrates asks, "What is justice?", it is not a prelude to giving the correct definition, but rather a first step toward appreciating how difficult and complex a question this is.

No.18
The Forms
Ideals in which all things participate

1/ Helicopter view: I might ask you to try to define something that we see every day – say, a table. You might point down at the one your papers are resting on. I would then respond that I didn't ask for an *example* of a table; I asked for the *definition* of a table. In other words, I asked for the *essence* of "table" – that which makes all examples of tables we see around us *be* what they are, as well as *be known* as what they are. You try again: a table is a space for supporting dinner plates or perhaps books. I would then point out that I can put all those things on the floor, and we don't call the floor a table, do we? You try again: a table has supports and holds up a surface, but I note that the very building in which we are standing has the same features. You start to get frustrated with me. But that's okay. It is actually very difficult to "get at" the definition of something, to see, grasp or understand its essence or nature. If you think tables are difficult, try defining other more complex things created by humans, or natural things such as astronomical, meteorological, chemical, atomic or subatomic phenomena that were "already there" before humans came along to define them. The Greek philosopher Socrates (*c.*470–399 BCE; see pages 38–9) apparently used to roam the city of Athens – accompanied by several younger followers, including Plato (428–348 BCE) – asking people frustrating questions such as "What's the essence of justice?"

What is the essential feature that makes an animal instantly recognizable as a dog?

2/ Shortcut: From Socrates' method, Plato inferred that there must be an actual realm of εἶδος (*eidos*) – which translates as "Forms" or "Ideas" – that humans can access through reasoning (in a similar way to the method we used in the table example opposite), where a thing's essence or nature exists perfectly. The objects we see around us in the visible world participate in the perfection of the Forms to various degrees. For example, dogs participate in the Form of Dog; just acts participate in the Form of Justice; and tables participate in the Form of Table.

See also //
17 Socratic ignorance, p.38
20 Knowledge, p.44

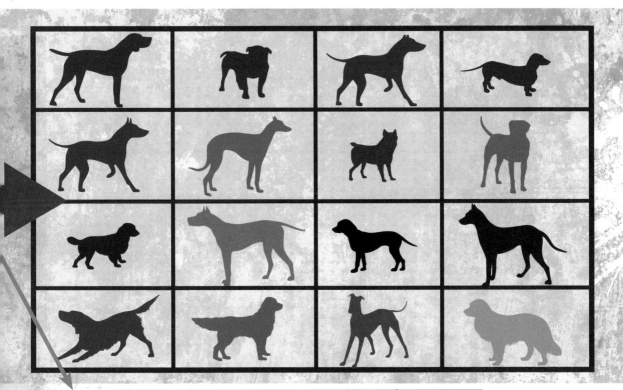

3/ Hack: Forms are in a separate realm that is only accessible through reason and act as the essences of things in the visible world we see, make things *be* what they are (through participation), and also be known as what they are (through philosophical discussion).

No.19
The Republic
Philosopher kings as charioteers

1/Helicopter view: In *Lord of the Flies*, the 1954 novel by Nobel Prize-winning author William Golding, a group of British boys become stranded on an island and start to murder one another before they are rescued. It is a glimpse into what life would be like if there were no laws governing social interaction. There's no doubt that humans need some kind of "law and order" imposed on social interaction to ensure peace, tranquillity and justice. But what exactly is justice? We seem to have an intuitive sense of justice. For example, we recognize injustice when someone pushes into a queue ahead of us when we've been waiting in that same line for an hour. So, justice seems to be equated with *fairness* of some kind, and we have all probably heard of distributive justice (concerning the fair allocation of goods and services in a social situation) and retributive justice (concerned with fair punishment for wrongdoing). The Greek philosopher Plato (428– 348 BCE) offers a theory of justice in *Republic*, his most famous social/ political work. He first argues that a human has three parts to their

personality: a base, desiring part; a spirited, semi-courageous part; and a rational part. And everybody is a bit different, with one part of his/her personality – their soul – dominating the other two.

2/Shortcut: Plato then extends his tripartite notion of the soul to the entire city. Justice, then, is defined as a harmonious relationship between the parts of the person or the parts of the city. When all the parts are "working together" – if you will – then you have justice. The ideal city is one where reason rules, with those rulers being the Philosopher Kings. The spirited, semi-courageous people are the police and military forces, while the base, desiring folks make up everybody else. Plato uses the parable of the chariot to illustrate his point: when the Charioteer (representing philosophy and the rational part of the psyche) is able to guide the two horses (representing the psychical elements of spirit and desire) appropriately, the chariot (the City) runs smoothly.

A scene from the 1963 film *Lord of the Flies* (left), a classic tale about the shallowness and fragility of the values underpinning human social life.

See also //

15 Striving for tyranny, p.34

88 John Rawls' original position, p.180

3/Hack: Plato's ideal Republic is one in which the Philosopher Kings, who are endowed with reason, rule and the city runs "smoothly", much like an expert charioteer can guide two horses smoothly.

No.20
Knowledge
Justified true belief

1/ Helicopter view: The following is an observation that I've heard many times: "Wow, that contestant on *Jeopardy!* really *knows* a lot!" However, I'm not sure the contestants on the game show are actually that knowledgeable. You might be wondering why I think this. Well, this brings us to the definition of knowledge, which is lodged in the philosophical realm of epistemology. The Greek words ἐπιστήμη (epistēmē) and λόγος (logos) can mean "knowledge, science or understanding" and "word, study or rational account", respectively, so *epistemology* refers to the study of knowledge. I think the contestants on *Jeopardy!* have good memories, but don't really know much about the subject matter related to their answers (or the questions). That's because we can define knowledge as (1) a belief that is (2) true and (3) justified. Looking at this in more detail: knowledge is (1) when you know something, you're said to believe it, meaning it is something you hold as a mental state in your head; (2) when you know something, what you know has to be true. You wouldn't say you know something

that's false, right; and (3) when you know something, you need to provide justification, and that means you must have *support* for your true belief. And you offer that support in the form of *evidence* of some kind. So, to know is to have a justified true belief.

2/Shortcut: The first person in the history of Western philosophy to treat knowledge as justified true belief was Plato (428–348 BCE) in his dialogue *Theaetetus*. In this dialogue, Plato has Socrates (470–399 BCE; see pages 38–9) and Theaetetus debate three definitions of knowledge, as follows: knowledge as being equated with perception; knowledge as being equated with true judgement (or belief); and knowledge as being equated with true judgement (or belief) with a justification (or an account). Interestingly, and what makes Plato an exceptional philosopher, is that each of these definitions is shown not to work and, in the end, we are left with ἀπορία, a philosophical "impasse" or "puzzlement" that essentially keeps the dialogue going to this day.

The Death of Socrates by David (1787) shows the philosopher speaking prior to drinking a cup of hemlock, his sentence passed by the Athenian court for impiety.

See also //
56 Not all swans are white, p.116
90 Edmund Gettier's Gettier Problem, p.184

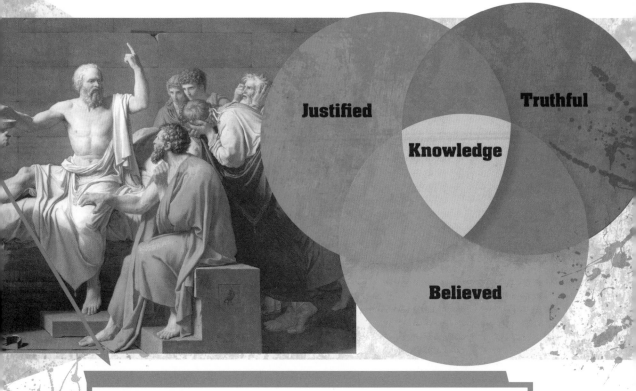

Justified

Truthful

Knowledge

Believed

3/Hack: The first person in the history of Western philosophy to treat knowledge as justified true belief was Plato in his dialogue *Theaetetus*.

No.21
Aristotle's hylomorphism

A different way to look at physical structures

Empedocles // c.490–430 BCE

1/Helicopter view: Hylomorphism (from the Greek words *hyle*, meaning "matter", and then *morphe*, meaning "form") was the central doctrine of Aristotle's philosophy of nature. According to the Greek philosopher, every natural body has two parts: firstly, what it is made of (which today we might speak of in terms of chemical elements and atomic structure) and, secondly, an actual form. A dog, or even a tree, for example, is much more than just certain materials arranged in a particular way.

To make sense of the underlying material part, Aristotle (384–322 BCE; see also pages 48–53) referred to the doctrine of the four elements – earth, water, air and fire – put forward by the Greek philosopher Empedocles (c.490–430 BCE), which was, during his time, the most detailed theory of physical substance. These four original elements still correspond in one sense to the chemical elements of modern science in as much as they cannot be broken down further (at least not in normal circumstances) and can combine to produce many different forms.

In this notion of change and flux, hylomorphism presages a living, quantum universe, rather than the dead, corpuscular one of atomic theory. Echoing older Eastern traditions, Democritus (c.460–370 BCE) and the atomists had described a universe consisting of just two fundamental principles: atom and void. The thrust of the theory is that matter is a passive receptacle from which form presses actual objects, things and beings. It is, in this sense, like much of Aristotle, a revisiting of the work of Plato (428–348 BCE; see pages 40–5).

The thrust of the theory of hylomorphism is that matter is a passive receptacle from which actual objects, things and beings emerge, in the same manner that a statue emerges from a block of stone.

2/ Shortcut: For centuries, atomism, mechanism and dynamism all rejected the hylomorphist's claim that real, intrinsic change can occur in the ultimate realities of the physical world, and reduced change to the superficial movements of inanimate particles in space.

Yet, today, modern physics, after being dominated by mechanism for 300 years, has returned to something closer in spirit to hylomorphism, with a renewed emphasis on the transmutability of mass into energy and vice versa, as well as on the "dance" of the subatomic world of protons, neutrons, electrons, mesons and other elementary particles.

See also //
22 Aristotle's Four Causes, p.48
51 René Descartes' substance dualism, p.106

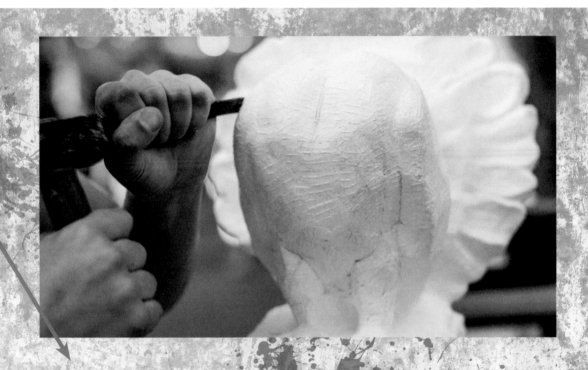

3/ Hack: In contrast to Democritus and the atomists, who explained the world of things in terms of varying arrangements of tiny particles, Aristotle makes the overall form primary, in the manner of a sculptor chipping away at a block of marble.

No.22
Aristotle's Four Causes
Revealing the unity of all things

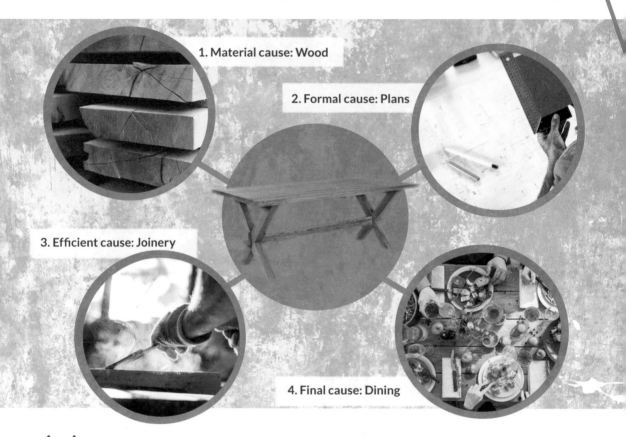

1. Material cause: Wood

2. Formal cause: Plans

3. Efficient cause: Joinery

4. Final cause: Dining

1/Helicopter view: The theory of the "Four Causes" put forward by Aristotle (384–322 BCE; see also pages 46–7 and 50–3) is just one part of an ambitious attempt to explain the workings of the physical world that is intended to shed light on the nature of change and the underlying unity of all things. Although the theory is invariably translated in terms of "causes", the word is misleading. In fact, the original Greek *aitia* might be better translated as "explanatory features" that provide insights into "why" things are as they are. Aristotle distinguishes four kinds of cause – material, formal, efficient and final (see page 80).

The schematic above illustrates Aristotle's different kinds of explanations as to why things are the way they are.

2/ Shortcut: The first of Aristotle's Four Causes is the most straightforward: merely relating to the matter of which a thing is made and the physical properties of that material. The second kind of cause, the formal, can perhaps be better understood as the account of "what-it-is-to-be". Consider the case of an apple tree: it has pink and white blossom of a certain kind and green and orange fruits of a certain kind *because* it is an apple tree.

See also //
21 Aristotle's hylomorphism, p.46
24 Aristotle's unmoved mover, p.52

Aristotle (right) // 384–322 BCE

The third of Aristotle's categories is usually summed up by the term "efficient", even though this does not correspond to any word that Aristotle himself uses. Perhaps a better way to think of this category is as the "source" of change – for example, the "efficient cause" of a statue is the sculptor.

The last category – the "final" cause – concerns the purpose or final end that is being sought. With that statue, for example, the final cause would not merely be the sculptor's desire to make something that looks like, say, a man throwing a spear, but might also be a desire to create something that celebrates the beauty of the human figure. Aristotle considered this kind of cause to be by far the most important and the one with the most explanatory power. The structure of an eye, for example, is to be explained ultimately in terms of it being a tool for human vision, rather than (as it might be) in terms of an evolutionary process in which certain cellular mutations proved to have useful consequences for an organism's survival.

3/ Hack: For Aristotle, a "cause" is an explanatory feature that both reveals and explains the fundamental nature of objects, creatures and phenomena.

No.23
Aristotle's happiness
What makes a plant happy?

1/ Helicopter view: For Aristotle (384–322 BCE; see also pages 46–9 and 52–3), happiness is not merely what we all seek, but what we all need in order to flourish and be properly human. The distinctive element in Aristotle's definition of happiness is that it is to be measured in terms of the proper functioning of the human animal.

Happiness, in this sense, is an optimal state and a complete good. The issue, really, is how to achieve that state. Aristotle considers various approaches. First of all, of course, there is the life of gratification, which revolves around pleasure-seeking and comfort. Not entirely the same, but obviously related, are lives dedicated to money-making and those dedicated to political action, whether as a means of achieving goals for the benefit of others or merely for the pleasure to be gained through the exercise of power. Finally, there is the approach favoured by the Eastern mystics and Aristotle's mentor, Plato (428–348 BCE; see pages 40–5), of the philosophical life – that is, the life of meditative contemplation and reflection.

At this point, Aristotle notes that what is necessary for a plant or, indeed, an animal to flourish is not the same as that required for a human being. This leads him to ask what is the key function of a human being? Aristotle, following Plato, thinks it must reside in our ability to think and reason.

2/Shortcut: Unlike Plato, Aristotle thinks that there needs to be some consideration of the goods people commonly find themselves desiring, since happiness lies in the attainment of our aims and desires. Aristotle divides these inspirational goods into three categories: (1) External goods (wealth, fame, honour, power and friends); (2) Personal goods (health, good looks, strength, athletic ability, and so on); and (3) Goods of the soul (knowledge, creativity, friendship, and so on).

Aristotle allows that things like life and health are necessary preconditions for happiness, while others, such as wealth or fame, are really only valuable in as much as they can facilitate other goals, before concluding that, ultimately, it is only in the exercise of *virtue* that we experience true happiness.

A lot hinges on your definition of virtue, however, and for Aristotle, at any rate, the virtuous life is not that of an ascetic studying books. In line with his method of surveying existing opinion and values, Aristotle praises rather the style of "The Great Man" who is good at everything and holds huge banquets at which he laughs heartily, while (no doubt) thumping the table with his wine glass and calling on the waiters for yet more roast meat.

The Triumph of Bacchus (c.1626–1628), by Velázquez, popularly known as *The Drinkers* (below), shows the pursuit of happiness through a life of gratification.

See also //

24 Aristotle's unmoved mover, p.52

25 Epicureanism and Stoicism, p.54

3/Hack: For Aristotle, happiness is about achieving your proper role and function in life. As to what that is, he uses conventional values as a guide and concludes that it requires both virtue and moderation.

No.24

Aristotle's unmoved mover

Applying earthly thinking to heavenly bodies

Aristotle // 384–322 BCE

1/ Helicopter view: The universe of Aristotle (384–322 BCE; see also pages 46–51), unlike the later Christian one, has no beginning in time and consists of circular motion, which is eternal. It is a universe rooted in the classical vision of rotating heavenly spheres. Aristotle conceived of several, not just one, first movers, which were somehow outside the universe, with no parts or magnitude.

Aristotle started from the belief that the Earth is itself fixed imperially and immobile at the centre of the universe, and that there was a vast circular movement of the heavenly firmament that could be seen at night whirling forever around. Secondly, he believed that the natural state of matter was to be at rest, unless something had obliged it to start moving. Thus, it was evident that something must have caused the heavens themselves to begin their grand rotation. He considers whether the cause might be physical, but rejects this possibility as every physical cause requires another one, and he objects to the idea of an infinite regress of additional causes. Aristotle uses the example of a stone moved by a man using a stick. It is not enough to say the stone is moved by the stick; it must be understood that the stick itself is moved by the action of a hand. Aristotle's First Mover is analogous to the immaterial human thought that starts the process that moves the hand.

Aristotle's belief is based on avoiding what he sees as logical contradictions. His first point is that moving things must be divisible and must have parts because the same thing cannot be both unchanged and changed all at once.

2/Shortcut: Sir Isaac Newton (1643–1727) demonstrated that bodies continue to move unless something opposes them. Thus, the universe could have been created with movement and has no need for an additional, exterior first mover or movers. However, Aristotle's mechanics were rooted in the understandable, but entirely false, idea that matter has a tendency to cease moving unless continuously propelled. In his work entitled *Physics*, Aristotle states, "Since motion must be everlasting and must never fail, there must be some everlasting first mover, one or more than one." In another work, *Metaphysics*, he describes the unmoved movers themselves as being immaterial substance: perfect, beautiful, indivisible and contemplating. He equates this entity with the active intellect.

See also //

22 Aristotle's Four Causes, p.48

37 Ultimate cause of everything, p.78

39 The Uncaused Cause, p.82

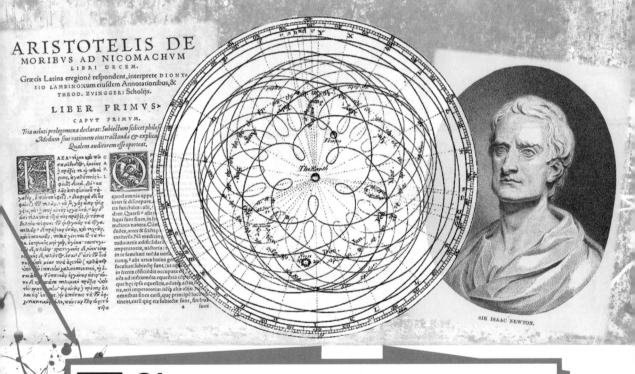

SIR ISAAC NEWTON.

3/Hack: Aristotle thought that all things are moved by something else. At the same time, it is impossible to have an infinite regress when considering the motion of finite things. The logical conclusion is that there must have been something to start the ball rolling.

No.25
Epicureanism and Stoicism
Pitting pleasure against pain

Epicurean philosophers Epicurus // 341–270 BCE
and his pupil Metrodorus // c.331–278 BCE

1/Helicopter view: Epicurus (341–270 BCE) founded a philosophical community in his garden, just outside the city walls of Athens, in Greece, at the end of the 4th century BCE. If his name has become synonymous with hedonism, it should be noted that he was, in fact, far more concerned with minimizing mental suffering than he was with maximizing bodily pleasures. Indeed, his aim was to free people from care, to achieve what the Greeks called a state of *ataraxia* ("tranquillity"). Epicureanism can be contrasted with another parallel movement of the time, the influential school of thought known as Stoicism (see page 76). However, the stress that the Stoics placed on overcoming pain and unhappiness through the development of self-control and fortitude perversely led the movement to actually seek out and embrace pain as a means of becoming more, well, stoical.

2/ Shortcut: Observing that mental disturbances are usually a greater obstacle to happiness than actual physical suffering, the Epicureans stressed that many human concerns, notably the fear of dying, are irrelevant to everyday life and instead recommended a focus on what might be called "objects of desire". These were divided between the categories of the natural and necessary (food and water); the natural but unnecessary (luxurious and fancy food); and the unnatural and unnecessary (social status and the trappings of great wealth). Following his own advice, Epicurus lived simply and put a high value on friendship.

The Epicureans argued that the pursuit of pleasure was, and should be, the ultimate aim of all human action. In making pleasure both a legitimate and central aim in life, Epicurus' teachings were in stark contrast with those of the Stoics, who insisted that only virtue could be considered properly good. If the Stoics accepted that, yes, it is better to be rich than poor, they still emphasized that neither condition should be able to affect your state of mind. Their stance was that emotions are an unhelpful encumbrance, which get in the way of sound judgements, and so should be overcome – essentially by ignoring them – and thus they were as much opposed to giving in to pleasure as they were to yielding to pain.

Jan Davidsz de Heem's *Still Life with Lobster* (1643) reflects later ideas of hedonism and bodily pleasure, yet Epicurus advocated living simply and seeking pleasure in friendship instead.

See also //

15 Striving for tyranny, p.34
23 Aristotle's happiness, p.50

3/ Hack: Both the Epicureans and the Stoics sought a path to mental tranquillity, the former by seeking a pleasant life and the latter by learning to ignore pain.

No.26

The Trinity
Three persons in one god

1/ Helicopter view: Religion emerges once a culture is settled and secure. Hinduism, for example, arose from the ancient Indus Valley Civilization (*c*.3300–1300 BCE), which extended from what is today northeast Afghanistan to Pakistan and northwest India. Now consider the peoples of the so-called Fertile Crescent, a historically significant region of the Middle East that included parts of present-day Egypt, Jordan, Lebanon, Palestine and Israel, among others. The people of the great civilization of Ancient Egypt, for example, were building the pyramids of Giza in around 2500 BCE. The Ancient Egyptians were polytheists – with gods such as Ra, Osiris, Anubis, Se and Atum – or, more precisely, they were henotheists (believing in many gods, but regarding one god as being more powerful than the rest). In contrast, Zoroastrians of the 2nd millennium BCE were theistic dualists, believing in two divine forces of good and evil, while the Ancient Israelites (*c*.1200 BCE) subscribed to what scholars say is one of the first true forms of monotheism, in which the divine is "Yahweh" – a One, Perfect, All-Knowing, All-Powerful, Supreme Being that is radically distinct and utterly "other" from anything in the universe. And yet, this Being created the universe – in short, brought this universe into being from/out of nothingness. Thus, for some 1,500 years, the Israelites and their descendants worshipped Yahweh as the One, True God.

Christians see the triangle as a representation of the trinity of the Father-Son-Holy Ghost but it has also represented the relationship of Father-Mother-Child, as well as symbolizing time as Past-Present-Future and the merging of Intellect, Love and Power.

2/ Shortcut: Into an Israelite world that worshipped Yahweh as the One, True God came Jesus of Nazareth (*c.*4 BCE–30 CE), the son of a carpenter. Jesus spent most of his adult life teaching and preaching around the Sea of Galilee, and maintained that he was the incarnation of the God of the Israelites, the "Son of the Father". But he also maintained that there was a third "person" in this Trinity, the Holy Spirit. Thus, Father, Son and Holy Spirit are three persons in One God. Yet, surprisingly (and perhaps confusingly), God is not *many* things or manifestations by virtue of this distinction. God is *homo/ousios,* meaning "one" in "being" (see page 59). Trying to make sense of this mysterious relationship, the Catholic patron saint of Ireland, St Patrick (402–491 CE), likened a shamrock – with its three distinguishable leaves that is yet one entire plant – to the Trinity.

See also //
**27 Arius'
Christology, p.58
28 Plotinus' three
hypostases, p.60**

3/ Hack: In Christian theology, the whole work of creation and miraculous redemption is understood as a single operation that has three aspects, revealed in three divine persons.

No.27
Arius' Christology
The father is greater than I

1/ Helicopter view: Jesus of Nazareth (*c*.4 BCE–30 CE) claimed that he was the incarnation of the God of the Jews/Israelites, the "Son of the Father" – and by this he meant more specifically that, "The Father and I are one" (John 10:30). Of course, this angered the Jews. Eventually, the Jews convinced Jerusalem's Roman leadership (namely, Herod Antipas and Pontius Pilate) to put Jesus to death by crucifixion. We are told in the New Testament Gospels that Jesus rose from the dead and ascended into Heaven. So, at the time, we can imagine people might have latched on to this event as a profound example of power, to be wanted and worshipped. Jesus had beaten death and he promised others that they too could beat death, essentially by living in Heaven with Him and His Father. They could achieve this if they followed his teachings. Christianity would spread even more rapidly following the Roman Emperor Constantine's proclamation of the Edict of Milan in 313 CE, which allowed Christians (and, in fact, any faith) to worship freely without persecution. With the spread of Christianity came more questions about the mysterious nature of Jesus' claim, "The Father and I are one." What did that mean exactly?

The First Council of Nicaea, shown in the icon above, sought to prove that Christ was equal to God.

2/ Shortcut: According to Arius (*c.*256–336 CE) – a priest in Alexandria, Egypt – because of the idea that God is a Perfect, All-Powerful, Supreme Entity, there could only be one such Being. Jesus was special, of course, in that he was the "first-born of all creation", and everything in the universe was created through Jesus; but he was certainly not equal to God. Arius pointed to Biblical passages in which Jesus makes statements such as, "The Father is greater than I" to bolster his position. Arius also argued that when Jesus said, "The Father and I are one", he was speaking more *figuratively*, whereas when he said, "I am the Son of God", that was a more accurate statement. The First Council of Nicaea in 325 CE was held specifically to refute "Arianism" (that is, Arius' Christology), with the bishops there declaring that Father, Son *and* Holy Spirit are three persons in One God or *homo/ousios*, which means "one" in "being" (see page 57) – who are all basically equivalent to one another.

The three images below are (left to right) an Orthodox icon of Jesus Christ "Pantocrator", the Pieter de Grebber painting *God Inviting Christ to Sit on the Throne at His Right Hand*, and a book engraving depicting Arius himself.

See also //
26 The Trinity, p.56
28 Plotinus' three hypostases, p.60

3/ Hack: According to Arius' Christology, because God is a Perfect, All-Powerful, Supreme Entity, there could be only *one* such Being, and so Jesus could not be equal to God.

Putting mind at the centre of the universe

 1/ Helicopter view: Plotinus' hypostases are one of the most obscure and mystical aspects of ancient philosophy. The word itself is derived from the Greek *hypostasis*, which means "underlying structures". The central idea is that of stages, or changes, in mind – not stages in individual human minds, but in some world or cosmic mind that later Christian thinkers tried to equate with their notions of "God", although this really wasn't Plotinus' intention.

Plotinus (*c.*205–270 CE) was born in Lyco, Egypt. It is thought that he travelled to the Far East with the Roman Emperor Gordian before returning to Europe at the age of around 40 and setting up a school in Rome. After entering a period of contemplation for about ten years, Plotinus set out his ideas, which, in mystic style, are presented as eternal truths and are not really open to debate.

The poetic phrase of the late Professor of Philosophy David W. Hamlyn, "like a dancer dancing the dance", describes how the world-soul orders the universe. Order emerges from the sequence of events.

2/Shortcut: Plotinus' central theme is that there are three aspects, or stages, to reality: the hypostases. These are visualized as a sort of circle, with the aim being to penetrate to the centre. Matter makes up the bulk of the universe, at the circumference of the circle, while the centre is pure mind. In between matter and pure mind lies the soul or "life", which is, of course, where we fit in.

See also //
6 Taoism's yin and yang, p.16
26 The Trinity, p.56

Plotinus stresses that the mind plays an active role in shaping or ordering the objects of its perception, rather than passively receiving the data of sensory experience. Mind is eternal and, in as much as humans possess a thinking part that participates in some (unexplained) way with the cosmic mind, we are eternal too.

There is a similar mystery surrounding the relationship of the soul – or, perhaps, a better term is "the life force" – with both the universe and the individual. There is a collective "world-soul", but this is divided between all individual things that have souls. The world-soul orders the universe, but not directly. It is rather, to use the poetic phrase of the late David W. Hamlyn, "like a dancer dancing the dance". It is this dance that gives us time. To quote directly from Plotinus' *The Enneads*:

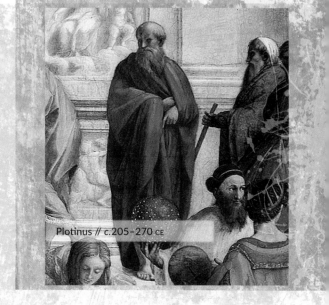

Plotinus // c.205–270 CE

"Now all life, even the least valuable, is an activity, and not a blind activity like that of flame…Life then aims at pattern as does the pantomimic dancer with his set movements; the mime, in himself, represents life, and, besides, his movements proceed in obedience to a pattern designed to symbolize life."

3/Hack: Plotinus' hypostases are obscure, but he is essentially saying that the objective world, including all our ideas of time, space, mass and so on, depends on consciousness, because we can never directly encounter reality. This can only be achieved through the mental models of reality that we create ourselves.

No.29
Porphyry's tree

A taxonomy of existence

 1/Helicopter view: People are "sorters" by nature. Throughout history we have formed systems of classification in an attempt to understand, explain, navigate, predict and control the complex workings of this universe. The Periodic Table of the elements used in chemistry comes to mind as a good example of one of these systems. In many ways, the contemporary classification techniques we utilize today in several areas of study and practice have their genesis in the common-sense ideas, arguments and methodologies of the Greek philosopher Aristotle (384–322 BCE; see pages 46–53). In his work titled *Categories*, Aristotle notes that we can basically partition things into ten categories of (1) substances of a certain kind, possessing inherent and transient (2) qualities, with properties such as (3) quantity, (4) time, (5) place, (6) position, (7) relationship to other things, (8) ownership, (9) activity and (10) passivity. Let's take the famous Greek philosopher Socrates (470–399 BCE; see pages 38–9) as an example. Socrates was a human being (1) who could become tanned by the Sun (2). He weighed 200lb/91kg (3), existed in 400 BCE (4) in Athena (5) and walked around the city (6) interacting with younger people (7), while wearing fancy sandals (8) and provoking lots of Athenians with his "method" (9), only to be brought to trial, found guilty and sentenced to death (10).

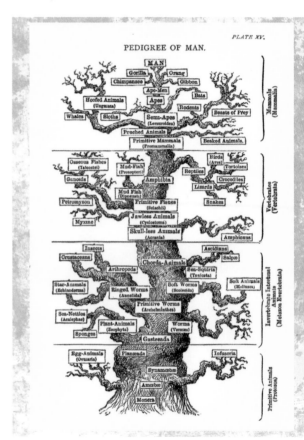

Ernst Haeckel's Tree of Life (1874) was inspired by Darwin's efforts to show the interrelated nature of all the planet's life forms.

2/Shortcut: A thinker called Porphyry of Tyre (*c.*234–305 CE) wrote a commentary on Aristotle's *Categories*. In his introduction, Porphyry sought to categorize all of reality into a genus/species dichotomy that later thinkers would illustrate as a kind of tree. At the top of the "tree" is a substance, either material or non-material – a material substance has a body, while a non-material substance does not. Material bodies are either living or non-living – living bodies are organisms, while non-living bodies are objects like rocks and minerals. Living, material organisms are either sentient (having one or more of the five senses), such as animals, or non-sentient, like plants. Sentient organisms are either rational/logical (humans) or non-rational/illogical (brute beasts).

An imagined debate between Averroës, a medieval Islamist philosopher, and Porphyry, as shown in a 14th-century manuscript (below).

See also //

18 The Forms, p.40
22 Aristotle's Four Causes, p.48

3/Hack: According to the Porphyrian Tree, all of reality is divided first into immaterial versus material substance, with material substance being further divided into the living and the non-living. The living are then divided into the sentient (animals) and the non-sentient (plants), and finally into the rationally sentient (humans) and the non-rationally sentient (brute animals).

Picture perfect?
Probably not, but beautiful nonetheless...

Primo Levi // 1919–1987

1/ Helicopter view: There is a major problem called *the problem of evil*, which exists if you look at the world and accept the reality that, on the one hand, horrendous evils have occurred (and still occur) as a result of humans and nature and, on the other hand, believe in the existence of a god that is all-knowing, all-powerful and all-good, who created the universe and cares for it, especially its human inhabitants. The One, Supreme God of Muslims, Christians and Jews has the aforementioned superlative and charitable features (despite numerous other theological, philosophical and cultural differences), and these monotheistic religions must also mount some kind of a response to the problem of evil. The Holocaust survivor Primo Levi (1919–1987) is famous for having summed up the sentiment of countless Jews and others regarding the Nazi death camps: "There is Auschwitz, and so there cannot be God." There have been different responses to the problem of evil, including what is known as the *free will defence* for human-caused evils: God gives people free will to choose even that which is absolutely despicable because to "step in" and treat us like puppets would be more despicable, more horrendous and more "evil" than the very evils we perpetuate.

Child concentration camp survivors at Auschwitz in 1945 (above).

2/ Shortcut: God gives humans free will, which works well for the so-called "evil that men do" – but what about those epidemics, cancers, deformities, abnormalities, plagues, hurricanes, earthquakes, tsunamis and other natural disasters that afflict humanity? The free will defence doesn't work for horrors such as those. Enter St Augustine of Hippo (354–430 CE), who is widely recognized as the Father of Medieval Philosophy and a major conduit for the development of Western theology and philosophy. In *De Civitate Dei* ("The City of God"), one of his famous works, Augustine tells us that, in the same way that the beauty of a picture is increased by virtue of an appropriate contrast of opposing light and dark shades, so, too, the "beauty of the universe becomes, by God's Ordinance, more brilliant by the opposition of contraries" of goodness and evil.

The Temptation of Christ (below left), a 19th-century painting by Franco-Dutch painter Ary Scheffer, illustrates the centrality of the notion of free will in ethics.

See also //

37 Ultimate cause of everything, p.78

93 Hannah Arendt's Banality of Evil, p.190

St Augustine // 354–430 CE

3/ Hack: It can be argued that suffering and evil are necessary in order to make possible free will and true goodness in the world.

No.31
Zen Buddhism's awakening *satori*
Seeking a path to enlightenment

 1/ Helicopter view: Zen is the Japanese name for a branch of Chinese Buddhism, formed in the 7th century CE, which is centred on achieving harmony with the Tao (the organizing principle of the

universe). The name comes from a Sanskrit term for meditation, and Zen practice involves both silent contemplation and the repeating of mystical sounds. The aim is to transcend the world of distinctions, including conceptual ones. Zen teachers may answer questions with paradoxical and enigmatic comments (or alternative questions) – consider, for example, the Zen Buddhist paradoxical riddle: "Who is it that responds, when your name is called?" Or they may simply refuse to speak.

The aim is always to avoid being caught in what Zen Buddhists consider to be a restrictive net of words. "Only not-thinking can tell thought anything helpful about how to get out of the way of itself", as the contemporary American aphorist, Alex Stein, has put it.

Similarly counterintuitive is the idea that the path to *satori*, which means "enlightenment" or "awakening", lies in carrying out life's daily tasks without any conscious effort to achieve enlightenment. Of course, this would appear to be an indistinguishable practice from the unenlightened life, too. Indeed, everyday activities are the same, but for the enlightened the actions have a different significance.

Strongly associated with Zen Buddhism, the *ensō* (circle) is hand-drawn in one or two uninhibited brushstrokes and symbolizes a moment when the mind is free to let the body create.

2/Shortcut: Adherents of Zen Buddhism say that to learn to act without conscious will or attachment is different from merely acting without conscious will or attachment – you have to know what you are missing to truly transcend it. It is a similar scenario for knowledge. The awakened one – as in the famous admission that is attributed to Socrates (470–399 BCE; see pages 38–9) – knows nothing, but this is very different from being in a state of mere ignorance. Rather, awakened people see that what they used to think of as problems are not real problems at all. Instead, they now transcend such issues and distinctions. This is highlighted in the Zen Buddhist saying: "The worldly self is *like a cupped handful of water.* We have it for as long as we can hold it."

See also //
1 Hinduism's theism, p.6
3 Brahman, p.10
32 Shintoism's *kami*, p.68

3/Hack: *Satori* ("awakening"), for the follower of Zen Buddhism, is the understanding that he/she is, and always has been, part of the Buddha nature, part of an all-encompassing shared reality.

No.32
Shintoism's *kami*
Breathing life into the inanimate

![馬遠]

1/Helicopter view: *Shinto* is a traditional Japanese religion that combines elements of folk practice with later Buddhist, Taoist and Confucian ideas. It has been practised since at least 500 BCE. The word *Shinto* itself means "Spirit path" or "Way of the Gods". Even among committed followers of the *Shinto* religion in Japan, there is great confusion over what kind of thing *kami* is. The obvious English translation is "spirits", but this can be misleading, as the Japanese concept covers much more than the English term would allow, including, for example, the elements of the landscape or the forces of nature. Indeed, *kami* can be a particular thing or merely a quality of something. The quality of "existence" is in this sense a kind of *kami*. The word *kami* itself gives few clues because it means only "that which is hidden".

An early 19th-century Chinese representation in ink on silk of "landscape" (above), one of the aspects of *kami*.

The *kami* spirit of the 9th-century CE Japanese poet, politician and scholar Sugawara no Michizane (right) is appealed to by Japanese students.

2/Shortcut: *Kami* can be many things, but if you think of them for the moment as a multitude of spirit forces, then they become a little like Western angels. Indeed, *kami* are supposed to have a particular interest in, and concern for, human beings, and may even respond to human prayers. They are believed to have the power to influence the course of natural forces and worldly events. And there are vast numbers of them; in fact, there is one *kami* for every possible object or situation. For example, there is a *kami* for education called *Tenjin*, who is associated with the spirit of the revered Japanese scholar Sugawara no Michizane (845–903 CE). Tenjin's help is often sought by Japanese students who are hoping for success in exams.

Three types of *kami* are considered to be particularly important. These are

(1) *Ujigami*, a type of *kami* who exerts a protective influence over members of a tribe, which can be thought of as the souls of ancestors;

(2) The *kami* of natural objects, such as mountains and rivers, or of the forces of nature, or of living creatures; and

(3) The *kami* of the departed, particularly the souls of human beings of particular note or achievement. However, it should be noted that, although many *kami* (called *musubi*) have a life-giving, positive influence and other *kami* (called *makoto*) have a sincere, truthful aspect, some *kami* are evil.

See also //
1 Hinduism's theism, p.6
3 Brahman, p.10
31 Zen Buddhism's awakening *satori*, p.66

3/Hack: Within Shinto, there is no rigid distinction between the material and the spiritual. Instead, the Shinto religion is based on belief in, and worship of, a multitude of spirit beings called kami that both influence and inhabit the material world.

No.33
Avicenna's Floating Man
An early experiment in sensory deprivation

 1/ Helicopter view: Avicenna (980–1037 CE) is the Latinized name of Ibn Sina, a medieval Islamic scholar and physician who was born in Persia. He is credited with introducing Aristotle (384–322 BCE; see pages 46–53), and hence much of Greek philosophy, to the Islamic world, while himself developing a mystical system based on a mixture of the works of Aristotle and Plotinus (c.205–270 CE; see pages 60–1), which presents God as a necessary being that created the universe by combining essence with existence. In the 12th and 13th centuries, the introduction of Avicenna's ideas had a profound effect on the development of Christian thought and, much later, on philosophy via the Jesuit scholastics. One likely example of this is Avicenna's thought experiment known as the "Floating Man". This seems to presage the later one by René Descartes (1596–1650; see pages 102–7) in a small, warm room heated by a bread oven in which Descartes imagines himself similarly disembodied and concludes that the only thing he can be sure of is an awareness of his own thoughts.

Experiments seem to show that if people are deprived of all sensory inputs, rather than settling into a wise, meditative state, as Avicenna suggests, they become disturbed and disorientated.

2/ Shortcut: Avicenna sets out his idea of the Floating Man in a work known as *The Book of Healing*, although this is not concerned with bodily medicine but rather with the safeguarding of the soul. There, he writes:

See also //
**49 René Descartes'
Evil Genius, p.102**
**50 René Descartes'
Cogito, p.104**

"One of us must suppose that he was just created at a stroke, fully developed and perfectly formed but with his vision shrouded from perceiving all external objects – created floating in the air or in the space, not buffeted by any perceptible current of the air that supports him, his limbs separated and kept out of contact with one another, so that they do not feel each other. Then let the subject consider whether he would affirm the existence of his self. There is no doubt that he would affirm his own existence, although not affirming the reality of any of his limbs or inner organs, his bowels, or heart or brain or any external thing… And if it were possible for him in such a state to imagine a hand or any other organ, he would not imagine it to be a part of himself or a condition of his existence."

The Floating Man thought experiment asks us to imagine what would remain if we were deprived of all sensory inputs. Indeed, there have been practical experiments that also investigate this, and what they seem to show is that rather than settling into a wise, meditative state, people become disturbed and disorientated instead. In this practical way, Avicenna's conclusion that the body is not really a necessary precondition for thought seems to be at least unproven.

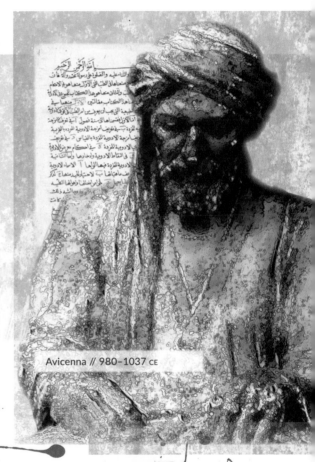

Avicenna // 980–1037 CE

3/ Hack: For Avicenna, the "Floating Man" thought experiment leads to the conclusion that the only things we truly know are our thoughts.

No.34
Averroës' eternal universe
Which came first, the cosmic chicken or the egg?

1/Helicopter view: Averroës (1126–1198) is considered to be one of the greatest Islamic philosophers of the medieval period. Nicknamed "The Commentator" because of his detailed writings on the Greek philosopher Aristotle (384–322 BCE; see pages 46–53), Averroës' thought has two related themes. First, he sought to clear away what he regarded as a pernicious, Neo-Platonic bias among his fellow philosophers and, second, he wished to promote a new account of Aristotle's own theories.

Averroës' starting point is to reject what he sees as philosophical compromises made in the name of theological orthodoxy. He prioritizes what he refers to as "demonstrative truth" (that is, logical or philosophical truth) over what he terms "dialectical" or "rhetorical" truth – incidentally, the word "dialectical" is not to be confused with how Karl Marx (1818–1883; see pages 142–3) later used the term.

One of the key philosophical points that Averroës sought to clarify was the question of whether the heavens were created or not. This led him to discuss and, indeed, to try to refute, the theory of the Persian philosopher Avicenna (980–1037 CE) that "essence precedes existence". On the contrary, for Averroës, existence must precede essence. This was, for him, a matter of recognizing the correct hierarchy of laws governing the universe. For, despite being entirely orthodox in his acceptance of the religious notions of divine revelation, Averroës insists that any proofs of God's existence must avoid metaphysical claims and rely on the science of physical causation alone. This, as always, was in line with Aristotle, whom Averroës also considered to have demonstrated the eternity of matter.

Averroës// 1126–1198

Medieval philosophers debated the origins of the universe, asking whether its beginnings should be accepted as an article of faith, or if they had to be demonstrable through logical argument.

2/Shortcut: Averroës says that the philosopher is not bound to accept what is contradicted by demonstration. With regard to the question of the origins of the universe, belief in the creation out of nothing must be abandoned because had not Aristotle demonstrated the eternity of matter and that creation is a continuing process? However, even if true to Aristotle, such an approach was too radical in his own time and place, and Averroës did not find many followers within Islam itself. His real influence was to come when Christian scholars in Europe rediscovered Greek philosophy through his writings.

See also //
2 Saṃsāra, p.8
37 Ultimate cause of everything, p.78

3/Hack: Averroës adapts Aristotle's argument that matter itself is the underlying substratum of all things, so it must have either created itself or have been eternal. Since, Aristotle and Averroës argue, the first is logically impossible, matter must therefore be eternal.

No.35
Moses Maimonides' negative theology
How not to talk about God

1/ Helicopter view: Negative theology sets limits on attempts to describe the Supreme Being, reasoning that finite human minds working within the limits of their languages cannot possibly approach, let alone appreciate, the full truth of the Creator. Although Clement of Alexandria (150–215 CE) is credited as the original proponent of this approach, Moses Maimonides (1135–1204), a Jewish lawyer and physician often known as Moses ben Maimon, is its most famous exponent.

Conventional philosophical and logical approaches would attempt to define and identify something by producing a list of its characteristics: God is good, God is omniscient, God is omnipotent, for example. But negative theology warns that such attempts always and inevitably introduce distortions and error. Even the most positive descriptions imply unwanted divisions. For instance, to say "God is good" is to introduce a gap between God and goodness. Other positive descriptions such as "God is all powerful" imply similarities with human capabilities and notions of power. Yet another problem is that statements about God, even ones like "God is pure goodness" or "God is everywhere and everything", constrain the infinite being, and so must be counted as false.

Moses Maimonides // 1135–1204

2/Shortcut: Underlying the approach of negative theology are two assumptions: first, that religious truth is non-cognitive and equivocal, and, second, that "what God is" must be what is left over when everything that can be put into words has been taken away. Even the most expansive statements about God's powers restrict the infinite being, and so must be regarded as untrue. Slowly recognizing the limitations of language in this way reveals a transcendent God whose complete "otherness" is safeguarded. However, by arguing both that positive statements about what God is are suspect and that the truth about God is essentially inexpressible, Maimonides was implying that the statements of the religious authorities themselves were suspect – a position that led to his writings being considered heretical.

A depiction of Maimonides from a medieval illuminated manuscript, in which he teaches students about the "measure of man".

See also //

39 The Uncaused Cause, p.82

48 Mulla Sadra's Illuminationism, p.100

 3/Hack: Religious texts are full of contradictions and impossibilities because they attempt to describe precisely what is indescribable.

No.36
The greatest being conceivable Hence, an existing being

1/Helicopter view: As Christianity spread throughout the Hellenic world during the 1st to 5th centuries, an increasing number of Church leaders were being educated in (or had already been educated in) Greek and Roman philosophy. Eventually, many of these philosophical ideas – most notably Neo-Platonism and Stoicism (see page 54) – were woven into Christian theology and morality by patristic thinkers such as St Justin Martyr (*c*.100–165 CE), St Clement of Alexandria (150–215 CE), Tertullian (*c*.155–240 CE), Origen (184–253 CE) and St Augustine of Hippo (354–430 CE; see page 65). Thus, in many ways, to understand the basic tenets of Catholic Christianity, one needs to understand these philosophical underpinnings.

Two important areas of philosophy that affected the theology of the Catholic Church as it grew during the Middle Ages were epistemology (see page 44) and metaphysics. The Greek words *epistēmē* and *logos* can mean "knowledge" and "word, rational account, or study of", respectively, so epistemology refers to the study of knowledge. The Greek words *meta* and *phusis* mean "beyond" and "nature", respectively, so the idea here is that *metaphysics* is the study of what goes *beyond* what we see in the natural world, so as to be an examination of the nature of existence itself. For Catholic thinkers during the Middle Ages, epistemology and metaphysics were intimately tied to one another, like two sides of the same coin. Into this tightly coupled relationship came St Anselm of Canterbury (1033–1109) with one of the cleverest arguments that trades in the epistemological and metaphysical realms.

2/ Shortcut: The Greek word *óntos* means "being", so *ontology* can refer to the study of being. In this sense, it is exactly the same thing as metaphysics. Anselm puts forward what later thinkers refer to as the *ontological argument for the existence of god*, which goes like this:

Premise 1: When you think of the concept of *god*, you think of the best or greatest conceivable being (of which no greater can be conceived).

Premise 2: It is "better" – meaning it has more existence, more "existential weight" – (a) to exist in the mind and in reality, than (b) to exist in the mind alone.

Premise 3: Remember, god is not merely a "better" being – god is the best being.

Conclusion: God must exist in the mind *and* in reality.

Scholastic philosopher St Anselm of Canterbury (left) and (below) a 16th-century portrayal of "God the Father", attributed to the Italian Renaissance painter Cima da Conegliano (1459–1517).

See also //
1 Hinduism's theism, p.6
3 Brahman, p.10
37 Ultimate cause of everything, p.78

3/ Hack: It is better to exist in the mind and in reality and, since god is the best being conceivable, god must exist not merely in the mind, but also in reality.

Ultimate cause of everything
Yet, not necessarily a direct cause

1/ Helicopter view: St Thomas Aquinas (1225–1274; see also pages 80–3) was a medieval scholastic (from the Latin *scholasticus*, meaning "of a school"), philosopher, systematizer, dialectician and harmonizer of Christianity with Aristotelianism and Neo-Platonism, who made essential contributions to what have become the official teachings of the Catholic Church concerning matters of faith and morals. A fundamental doctrine of Christianity (and of Islam and Judaism, too) with which Aquinas was concerned is *creation ex nihilo*, the idea that God, being One, Supreme and, in short, Perfect, is all that existed at one point. God then created the universe out of nothing (since there was nothing there except God). Now, this presents us with a serious problem – namely, if God is the cause of the universe, the question arises as to whether God is the *ultimate cause of everything* that occurs in the universe. And if that's the case, then that would make God the being *ultimately responsible for everything that occurs in the universe.* And if that's the case, then one major problem is that it would be difficult to hold humans responsible for their actions.

St Thomas Aquinas (above), the 13th-century Dominican friar who set out the "Five Ways" in which God's existence could be proved.

2/ Shortcut: Aquinas' response to the question of whether humans are responsible for their actions is that, although God is the ultimate, first or primary cause of all things, he has created humans and natural entities such that they can engage in actions and processes, begetting their own causal chains in a subordinate, secondary fashion. So, God is the remote source of all things that cause other things to occur or act in a certain way, and so on. By analogy, the proud and honest car manufacturer constructs a car that is as good as it can possibly be, but it is still prone to breaking down or malfunctioning, given the workings and interactions of the parts. Furthermore, someone may drive the car and not take care of it, or run it into a tree because he or she has been drinking. The car manufacturer is not directly responsible for any of the evils that result from the workings of the car or the actions of the driver.

Michelangelo's painting on the ceiling of the Sistine Chapel in Rome (below) depicts God creating Adam.

See also //

1 Hinduism's theism, p.6

3 Brahman, p.10

36 The greatest being conceivable, p.76

3/ Hack: Although God is the ultimate, first or *primary* cause of all things, he has created humans and natural entities such that they can engage in actions and processes, begetting their own causal chains in a subordinate, *secondary* fashion.

No.38
The theological doctrine of transubstantiation
Putting Aristotle's Four Causes to good philosophical work

 1/ Helicopter view: *Crede, ut intelligas* (meaning "Believe, so that you may understand") is what St Augustine of Hippo (354–430 CE; see page 65) tells us in his *Tractates on the Gospel of John*, and he was one of many theologians who used reason, as well as the arguments and ideas of philosophers, to try to make sense of his faith. Augustine drew a great deal on the Greek philosopher Plato (428–348 BCE; see pages 40–5) and thinkers known as Neo-Platonists. Thus, given Augustine's influence on the theology and philosophy of the Catholic Church in the Early Middle Ages, Plato's thinking was the dominant philosophical point of view. That all started to change with St Albert Magnus/the Great (*c.*1200–1280) and his student, St Thomas Aquinas (1225–1274; see pages 78–9 and 82–3), both of whom were enthralled by Aristotle (384–322 BCE; see pages 46–53). Of course, Aquinas' acceptance of Aristotle (as well as of Plato and any relevant thinker) was always within the context of his Catholic faith, and always with the intention of making sense of that faith and justifying it rationally. Possibly the most powerful of Aristotle's ideas borrowed by Aquinas comes from Aristotle's *Physics* 2.3 and *Metaphysics* 5.2: the doctrine of the Four Causes – material, formal, efficient and final. Aquinas was able to use the Four Causes to explain several concepts and positions within the Catholic faith.

Detail of the Italian fresco *Triumph of St Thomas*, attributed to the 14th-century painter Andrea di Bonaiuto of Florence (above).

2/Shortcut: Aquinas used Aristotle's doctrine of the Four Causes to explain several positions in the Catholic faith. One of those positions is the doctrine of transubstantiation, which is the *trans*formation of the *substance* of bread and wine into the *real* body and blood of Christ at the moment of consecration, with only the appearances of bread and wine still remaining. The *material* cause is the bread and wine, which, like prime matter, stays the same throughout the change in consecration (that's why the bread and wine *look/appear* the same before and after). The *efficient* cause is the priest, who consecrates the bread and wine. The *final* cause is the end or reason why the consecration is taking place, and that is to do with human salvation, going back to what Jesus communicated at the Last Supper. And the *formal* cause is the *real presence* of Jesus in the bread and wine.

A detail from Leonardo da Vinci's imagining of the Last Supper (below left); and part of a Catholic church ritual representing transubstantiation (below right).

See also //

22 Aristotle's Four Causes, p.48

26 The Trinity, p.56

3/Hack: Aquinas was able to use Aristotle's doctrine of the Four Causes to explain the Catholic doctrine of transubstantiation.

No.39
The Uncaused Cause
A self-sufficient source of existence

 1/ Helicopter view: We have all wondered at one point or another, "What caused the universe?" If you're a naturalist in the realm of philosophy or science, then you believe that observable events in the universe are fully explainable by natural causes without reference to the supernatural. Indeed, you think that the universe is *self-explanatory, in principle,* even if we haven't found the *ultimate* explanation just yet. After all, the Big Bang is the answer to the question, "What caused the universe?" We can then continue questioning and ask, "What caused the Big Bang?", and what caused that, and so on. However, many people have found this persistent questioning to be unsatisfactory as an explanation. Aristotle (384–322 BCE; see pages 46–53) thought that finding a complete explanation for causation within the universe had to appeal to something *wholly distinct* from the universe, a kind of Prime Being that is not subject to any causes itself – in other words, an Uncaused Cause. An ultimate explanation for the various entities and processes of our experience leads us to the recognition that there is some being that is the source of the universe, but which cannot be subject to the same laws, processes, motions, causes and other natural processes of the universe.

The Uncaused Cause is something wholly distinct from the rest of the universe, a kind of Prime Being that is not subject to the same laws.

2/ Shortcut: If you're a religious person, the Uncaused Cause discussed by Aristotle could easily be a god, and that is exactly how St Thomas Aquinas (1225–1274; see pages 78–81) viewed the situation. In fact, Aquinas is famous for his *quinquae viae* (meaning "five ways or proofs") for the existence of God, which he lays out in his famous tome, *Summa Theologica,* at Part I.2.3 ("Whether God exists?"). The proof of the Uncaused Cause is the second of the five that he mentions there. This general approach, which was used by Aquinas to move from the observation of things in the universe to a cause that exists behind/beyond the universe, has become known as a *cosmological argument for the existence of God*, from the Greek *kosmos*, meaning "ordered universe".

See also //

22 Aristotle's Four Causes, p.48

24 Aristotle's unmoved mover, p.52

3/ Hack: Aquinas argues that an ultimate explanation for causality in the universe leads to a source outside the universe that is itself uncaused – in other words, an Uncaused Cause. Otherwise, it would be *yet another* thing in the universe that is in need of an explanation.

No.40

John Duns Scotus' voluntarism

In praise of freedom

John Duns Scotus // 1266–1308

Johannes Duns Scotus, Doctor Subtilis

1/ Helicopter view: As his name helpfully suggests, John Duns Scotus (1266–1308) was Scottish and, indeed, probably came from Duns, although he studied at the University of Oxford and lectured in Paris. His name is also the source of the word "dunce", meaning a very ignorant or stupid person – an unkind slander that arose as a result of his intellectual dispute with the teachings of St Thomas Aquinas (1225–1274; see pages 78–83) over the nature of what is actually possible. The term "voluntarism" itself relates to a religious debate about the constraints that the universe places, not only on human choices, but on God too.

In addition, Duns Scotus sought to demonstrate that morality comes from God's will and his choices rather than via his intellect or knowledge. Similarly, Duns Scotus argued that human volition (or decision-making) is distinct from the intellect, and not bound by it. This is a powerful insight, even for non-believers.

2/ Shortcut: Duns Scotus' most ambitious project was to demonstrate the primacy of free will, against those who spoke of a universe where it appeared that humans were only responding to other forces. It seemed to him that even the Creator was too often constrained, particularly by the laws of logic and time. Can God change the past? Can God will two things that are mutually exclusive? As to this last challenge, Duns Scotus is emphatic, arguing that God *can*, for example, both love and hate something at the same moment. For medieval theologians the divine will *had to be able to do this* otherwise it would be limited.

The argument Duns Scotus offers is taken from Aristotle (384–322 BCE; see pages 46–53), and relates to time. Consider the sentence, "A sitting man can run." Of course, this is false if it is taken to refer only to the present instant – but it is true if we allow that, at a later time, the sitting man can stand up and, well, run. The fact that the "sitting man" can choose to run later illustrates the existence of what Duns Scotus calls "real possibility".

The schematic below illustrates the idea that human freedom consists of being able to choose.

See also //

37 Ultimate cause of everything, p.78
57 David Hume's compatibilism, p.118

3/ Hack: In philosophy, voluntarism stresses the unlimited nature of the divine will and argues for an expanded range of human freedom.

No.41
William of Ockham's
nominalism Words as signposts

1/Helicopter view: William of Ockham (*c.*1287–1347; see also pages 88–9) was an English monk who is best known for the eponymous "Ockham's Razor", a logical rule of reasoning that is also referred to as the "Technique of Parsimony". Another aspect of the Razor was an emphasis on "nominalism", and with the appropriateness of our use of language. Nominalism insists that when we call things "chairs", for example, this is simply because they all conform to the rules governing the use of the word "chair", rather than having some strange quality of "chair-ness", perhaps, as Plato (428–348 BCE; see pages 40–5) imagined, being drawn from the ideal world of the Forms. A general term, or what philosophers call a universal term, is a sign that points at many individual things that share some quality.

William of Ockham // *c.*1287–1347

2/ Shortcut: Ockham was, indeed, an early semiologist, or scientist of the use of signs, distinguishing between intuitive "signs", which are words for "labelling" impressions derived from the senses, such as "hot", "yellow" or even "dog", and mental signs, such as "all" in the sentence, "All men are rational", which are abstract and suitable for philosophical manipulation. Words such as "all", he warns, are meaningless in themselves and must only be allowed as mental short-cuts for longer – perhaps impractically long – sentences that really do describe the world directly.

Of course, as with all things linguistic, the distinctions are not at all clear-cut. Someone might use the word "dog" while pointing in a very concrete way at such an animal, which is for Ockham how words really should be used, but he or she might also use the word "dog" as a general term, or what philosophers call a "universal", by saying, for example, "If it is a dog, then it will chase the cat."

Ockham extended this idea to numbers, rejecting not only, for example, the number 17 itself as a thing, but also other mathematical objects such as lines or points. These are useful as concepts, but do not have a separate existence apart from their earthly approximations.

Scenes from an imagined agricultural calendar from a 1306 manuscript of Pietro Crescenzi (below). Each image is a kind of sign, conveying information.

See also //

20 Knowledge, p.44
42 William of Ockham's "Razor", p.88
77 Perceiver, perception and perceived, p.158

3/ Hack: For Ockham, only specific things exist and the categories we invent are mere words that point at these particulars.

No.42
William of Ockham's "Razor"
In praise of simple explanations

1/ Helicopter view: William of Ockham (*c.*1287–1347) was an English monk, nicknamed the "More than Subtle Doctor". He was immortalized as a result of a rule of reasoning called the "Razor", which was named after him and is also known as the "Technique of Parsimony". The Razor simply states that given a range of possible explanations, the most simple is to be preferred. Or, in a translation closer to the Latin original, *Entia non sunt multiplicanda sine necessitate* ("that one should not multiply entities beyond the necessary"). The implication is that you should always prefer the explanation that relies upon the fewest possible number of causes, factors or variables.

A sketch labelled *Frater Occham iste* in a manuscript of Ockham's *Summa Logicae* (*The Logic Handbook*), which is dated 1341.

2/ Shortcut: William of Ockham was the forerunner of much of the philosophy of language that was developed later, and influenced other English philosophers such as Thomas Hobbes (1588–1679; see pages 96–7) and John Locke (1632–1704; see pages 112–13). Although in many ways Aristotelian, Ockham's Razor reflects a divergence with Aristotle (384–322 BCE; see pages 46–53) who had freely generated new categories and distinctions.

Considerable achievements have been claimed as a result of applying Ockham's clear thinking. For example, Ockham's critique of the Ancients' concept of matter as "potentiality" encouraged René Descartes (1596–1650; see pages 102–7) to describe it as simply "extension", and also ushered in a distinction between "primary" and "secondary" qualities. In logic, Ockham added to the two usual values of "true" and "false" a third possibility, that of being "indeterminate". This only really became important for mathematics in the 20th century, making it remarkable that Ockham had detailed it 600 years earlier. Likewise, when Ockham challenged Aristotle's notions of "final causes" and "essences", he prepared the ground for the Scientific Revolution (see pages 94–5) of the 15th, 16th and 17th centuries.

There is something subversive about Ockham's approach and, indeed, many of the conclusions that he came to challenged the conventional opinions of the time. Differences with the Church led to him being excommunicated in 1328, although he successfully sought refuge in France and Germany. He remained active in his research into his early sixties when – satisfactorily in the eyes of his critics, who read it as a confirmation of his fall from grace – he contracted the Black Plague and died.

See also //

41 William of Ockham's nominalism, p.86

45 Francis Bacon's gift to science, p.94

67 Auguste Comte's positivism, p.138

multipliranda sine necessitate

3/ Hack: Ockham's influence is the idea that one should always be biased toward simplicity when constructing a theory. However, he was aware that nature does not always follow the simplest course, and was himself prepared to invent new terms – where they really did seem necessary.

St Teresa of Ávila's grace

Looking inward

St Teresa // 1515–1582

1/Helicopter view: St Teresa of Ávila (1515–1582) was a Spanish Carmelite nun, mystic and author who lived during the Counter-Reformation. Although canonized by Pope Gregory XV in 1622, some 40 years after her death, it wasn't until 1970 that Teresa's scholarly writings were honoured when she was named a Doctor of the Church by Pope Paul VI. Her books include an autobiography, *El Castillo Interior* (usually translated, rather inelegantly, as "The Interior Castle") and *Camino de Perfección* ("The Way of Perfection").

Within theology, Teresa's influence is to assert the importance of God's grace, which is the love and mercy given to us by God because He desires us to have it, not necessarily because of anything we have done to earn it. Teresa uses the metaphor of grace as a kind of rain that gently nourishes the world.

This image of St Teresa was painted by the 17th-century Spanish artist Alonso del Arco and emphasizes her mystical quality through the indicated communion with a white dove.

2/Shortcut: Christia Mercer, a contemporary philosophy professor at Columbia University, in New York, claims that René Descartes (1596–1650; see pages 102–7) lifted some of his most influential ideas from Teresa, whose books on the role of philosophical reflection in intellectual growth appeared some 70 years before Descartes'. Mercer argues that there are a number of striking similarities between Descartes' *Meditations on First Philosophy* and Teresa's *Interior Castle*. She believes that Descartes borrowed from Teresa when he argued that prolonged periods of introspection are necessary in order to shed one's personal biases and gain a clearer perspective on the world. To quote from Teresa's book:

See also //
26 The Trinity, p.56
37 Ultimate cause of everything, p.78

"I do not know whether I have put this clearly; self-knowledge is of such consequence that I would not have you careless of it, though you may be lifted to heaven in prayer, because while on earth nothing is more needful than humility."

Descartes never mentions – let alone credits – Teresa, and subsequent commentators have dismissed her as a mystic. As Mercer says, "Many women of her time who wrote about philosophical matters were labelled as 'mystics' and disregarded by the academy." Having said that, Descartes might well have been sceptical about some of the claims made about Teresa following her death, including that on being exhumed her body was found to be miraculously intact and exuding a scent, like perfume.

3/Hack: Teresa stresses that the initiative of grace is always on the side of God, while a complaint sometimes made about more liberal approaches is that they exaggerate the ability of an individual to decide their own fate and to effect their own salvation entirely apart from God's grace.

Machiavelli's Prince
Better to be feared than loved

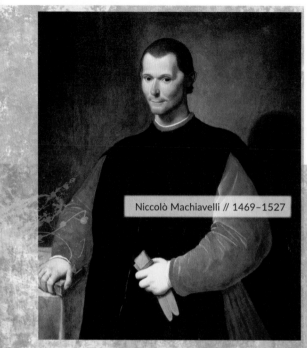

Niccolò Machiavelli // 1469–1527

1/ Helicopter view: The Golden Rule – "Do unto others as you would have them do unto you" – is a staple of Confucianism, Judaism, Christianity, and many religious and secular moral systems.

One cardinal virtue and important tenet of Hinduism, Buddhism and Jainism is *ahimsa*, the belief that one should never injure another being. Now, picture a school playground. Sally hits Johnny and Johnny retaliates by kicking her, and they are both punished by the teacher. But then we grow up. And we realize that a lot of the adults who told us that we should never lie, cheat or steal are, in fact, liars, cheats and thieves themselves. We realize that to be able to negotiate our way in the world and get what we want may require that we lie, cheat or steal at times. And then, when we look at people who have more responsibility and power, we realize that they are capable of even more egregious acts, such as torture, rape and murder. It may shock us to realize too that, at times, religious people are perpetuating these acts. The history of philosophy, theology and religion all around the world is filled with textbooks and guidelines about how to live good, virtuous, upright, just and moral lives. We can consider these the moral "self-help" books of their day. But a moral self-help book that advocates being vicious, if necessary?

Machiavelli in Santi di Tito's famous portrayal of the philosopher and writer (above).

2/Shortcut: A moral self-help book that advocates being vicious is what Niccolò Machiavelli (1469–1527) produced when he penned *Il Principe* (*The Prince*), which was published in 1532. This work infamously answered the question, "Is it better to be feared or loved?" with a response that, given the impossibility of being both and the fact that a prince has to rule over many people who are out for their own benefit, it is better to be feared. Machiavelli also advised that, if you want to be a successful prince, then you have to "keep up appearances" – try to be virtuous, but be vicious if need be, and aim to keep your word, but again, lie if it helps you.

Cesare and Lucrezia Borgia, progeny of Pope Alexander VI, whose love of power was the subject of Machiavelli's philosophy (below).

See also //
15 Striving for tyranny, p.34
19 The Republic, p.42
23 Aristotle's happiness, p.50

3/Hack: In *The Prince*, Machiavelli answers the question, "Is it better to be feared or loved?" with a response in favour of being feared.

No.45
Francis Bacon's
gift to science The scientific method

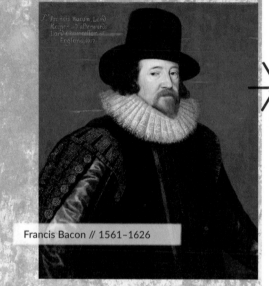

Francis Bacon // 1561–1626

1/ Helicopter view: One basic meaning of the English word "science" is traceable through 14th-century Old English and 12th-century Old French to Latin, and it is "knowledge". For Aristotle (384–322 BCE; see pages 46–53), science is the search for universal truths concerning the causes of things. However, these causes are revealed, not through empirical observation, but through the rigorous application of sound deductive reasoning. Science progresses through the practice of logic – specifically, categorical logic – and not by means of experimentation. Empirical evidence may be where one starts the investigation and it may certainly suggest generalizations, but, says Aristotle, it cannot reveal the causes of things. The mind must abstract universal natures (that is, types, kinds) from observations of particular things and work with those in a purely mental way.

Experimentation of the sort commonly associated with modern science actually emerged in the Middle East in the works of Ibn al-Haytham (Alhazen; 965–1040 CE), Al-Biruni (973–1048 CE) and Ibn Sīnā (Avicenna; 980–1037 CE), all of whom, interestingly enough, wrote commentaries on Aristotle. The 1543 publication of Nicolaus Copernicus' *De revolutionibus orbium coelestium* ("On the Revolutions of the Heavenly Spheres") is often cited as marking the beginning of the Scientific Revolution of the 15th, 16th and 17th centuries. And it was this Revolution in Western Europe that would lay the bedrock foundations for the various sciences that exist today.

2/ Shortcut: Possibly the most important figure of the Scientific Revolution was the so-called Father of the Scientific Method, Francis Bacon (1561–1626), an English scientist, lawyer, statesman and philosopher. In his famous work, *Novum Organum Scientiarum* ("New Instrument of Science"), Bacon lays out the basics of the Scientific Method that we know today: observe, hypothesize, predict, test and modify. The title is a reference to Aristotle's *Organon*, a treatise on logic and syllogism, which were the instruments Aristotle used in his scientific approach. The idea in *Novum Organum Scientiarum* is that Bacon is describing a new method for gaining knowledge, complete with new instruments and a new system of logic that he believes to be superior to Aristotle's.

This series of photographs is part of Eadweard Muybridge's 19th-century experiment into whether or not a galloping horse always keeps one hoof on the ground.

See also //

82 Karl Popper's falsifiability, p.168

83 Shifting paradigms, p.170

3/ Hack: Francis Bacon laid out the basics of the Scientific Method that we know today: observe, hypothesize, predict, test and modify.

Thomas Hobbes // 1588–1679

Hobbes' *Leviathan*

Contract and live in peace or die in the state of nature

1/ Helicopter view: In his work *Politics*, Aristotle (384–322 BCE; see pages 46–53) taught that humans are naturally communal beings who simply want to gather together and form laws and rules in societies. He believed this because he regarded humans as rational animals. For sure, there are those in social situations who, at times, act more in line with their animal side, and they need to be punished. However, most human beings are reasonable and good-natured, and even want to work with others for the common good. If we fast-forward the history of the West to a Christian thinker like St Augustine of Hippo (354–430 CE; see page 65), it can be seen that, in spite of the doctrine of Original Sin, humans still have an innate desire for the goodness associated with God, redemption and social interaction. But then came events in medieval human history such as the various Crusades and Inquisitions – in which thousands upon thousands of people were tortured and slaughtered – and nefarious people like Genghis Khan (1162–1227) and Vlad the Impaler (1427–1476) who committed atrocities in a way that struck a nerve with thinkers. And they started rethinking the goodness and sociability of humanity.

The frontispiece of *Leviathan* by Thomas Hobbes (right). The book was so controversial that its publication was cited by the British Parliament as a possible cause of the Great Fire of London in 1666.

See also //
19 The Republic, p.42
69 Karl Marx's *Communist Manifesto*, p.142
88 John Rawls' original position, p.180

2/Shortcut: Thomas Hobbes (1588–1679) lived through three-quarters of the Stuart dynasty (1603–1714), a time in British history that witnessed not only one Cromwell, two kings called Charles and at least three civil wars, but also a great deal of butchery, beheadings and bloodshed. So, it's no wonder that Hobbes diagnosed the human condition as being one of a state of nature – "man to man is an errant wolf", people are selfish, and pleasure and pain ultimately guide all our actions. The scene is very *unlike* Aristotle's natural state of camaraderie, and if we have any hope of our lives being anything other than "solitary, nasty, brutish and short" (to use Hobbes' own words), then we have to make a *contract* with one another – literally – and agree to put someone, or something, in power to keep us in line, no matter what. The massive ruling power that we bring into being can be likened to a *leviathan*, a great sea monster that is spoken of in the Hebrew Scriptures – our self-imposed salvation.

3/Hack: If people want any semblance of civility, they must make a contract with one another and agree to put a massive power in place – a leviathan – that will govern with enough force to keep them from killing each other.

No.47
Pascal's Wager

Betting on the existence of God

Blaise Pascal // 1623–1662

 1/Helicopter view: If you've ever engaged in activities such as dice rolling, card playing and the spinning of the roulette wheel, even for a short period of time, it is not hard to imagine that it was gambling that led to serious advances in statistics and probability theory. Gather a group of smart people around a card table for a game of poker, for example, and eventually the *really* smart ones will start to "count cards" – which is illegal in gambling establishments – and "guesstimate" what will be dealt to them next. That's exactly what the polymath Blaise Pascal (1623–1662) was apparently able to do when he played cards with his friends, including Pierre de Fermat (1607–1665), a famous mathematician who made significant contributions to probability theory, geometry, number theory and infinitesimal calculus. And Pascal didn't simply play the roulette wheel – he *invented* it. Gambling and probability go together and make sense – but gambling and God? After converting to Catholicism in his twenties, Pascal began thinking seriously about atheism, agnosticism and notions of the afterlife, either in Heaven with God or in Hell without God. Eventually, these ideas would be posthumously organized and published as his *Pensées* (*Thoughts*), with the most-oft-cited portion of the collection being Pascal's famous "Wager".

Pascal intended his "Wager" to be put at the beginning of his book, not to settle the question of how to live one's life but instead to show that logical reasoning cannot convincingly settle the issue and that we must look elsewhere for insights.

2/Shortcut: Pascal's wager goes like this. First, here are the possible options for this life and what may happen in the "next life":

See also //
39 The Uncaused Cause, p.82
100 The prisoner's dilemma, p.204

1 Live like a Catholic, take the sacraments and do God's will. Then, you die and it turns out that there is a God and you get to go to Heaven. *This is a big reward. You want this!*

2 Live like a sinner, shun Catholicism and don't do God's will. Then, you die and it turns out there is a God and you get to go to Hell. *This is a big punishment. You don't want this!*

3 Live like a Catholic, take the sacraments and do God's will. Then, you die and it turns out there is no God and no Heaven. *But…if you're wrong, no big deal. No big reward and no big punishment.*

4 Live like a sinner, shun Catholicism and don't do God's will. Then, you die and it turns out there is no God and no Heaven. *But…if you're wrong, big punishment!*

Pascal then concludes that, given these options, 3 is the most significant and, regardless of whether God exists, Catholics (and theists, in general) have it better than atheists. Thus, it is better to "place your bet" on belief in God.

3/Hack: Pascal thinks we should wager that there is a God because if there is a God, you go to Heaven. If there isn't a God, then you're not losing out as much as the atheist who chooses not to believe in God when it turns out that there is, in fact, a God all along (because the atheist goes to Hell).

No.48

Mulla Sadra's Illuminationism

The special place of light in philosophy

Avicenna // 980–1037 CE

1/ Helicopter view: The philosophy known as Illuminationism really goes back to well before Plato (428–348 BCE; see pages 40–5), but is particularly associated with Islamic philosophers writing in the medieval period. The approach emphasizes intuition over empirical investigation, and "essence" over "existence". The intention, however, is to unite both worlds. Sadr al-Din al-Shirazi (*c.*1571/2–1640), who is usually referred to as Mulla Sadra, is counted as a master of the Illuminationist (or *Ishraghi* or *Ishraqi*) school and also as the most influential Islamic philosopher of the last 400 years. An Iranian Shia theologian, he wrote over 40 works, which attempt to synthesize multiple philosophical traditions from the Islamic Golden Age in order to create what he hoped would be a new metaphilosophy that he called "Transcendent Theosophy" (or *Al-hikmah al-muta'liyah*).

Avicenna and illuminations from his *The Canon of Medicine* (above).

2/Shortcut: The term "Illuminationism" seems to have been first used by the Persian philosopher Avicenna (980–1037 CE; see pages 70–1), who describes Eastern insights as a source of superior wisdom to Western rationalism. A century later, Suhrawardi (1155–1191), the founder of the Persian school of Illuminationism, mocked the efforts of the Western philosophers to explore reality as being like "seeking the sun with a lamp", but spoke approvingly of Plato, whom he called "the inspired and the illumined", as well as "the guide and master of philosophy". At the heart of Plato's writing is the idea that "the Good" can be compared to "Light", and that knowledge is comparable to illumination.

Text from the Egyptian–Greek *Corpus Hermeticum* (below).

For the school's medieval followers, the true path starts somewhere in the East, then travels to Ancient Persia before being picked up by the Egyptian mystic Hermes Trismegistus and Plato. Hermeticism emerged in Late Antiquity in parallel with early Christianity and several other esoteric doctrines, which were all characterized by efforts to unite rationality and doctrinal faith. The texts known as the *Corpus Hermeticum* (2nd century CE and later) stress the oneness and goodness of God, and the need for purification of the soul. Within them, too, light is divided into different kinds, one of which is akin to the immortal soul.

See also //
35 Moses Maimonides' negative theology, p.74
39 The Uncaused Cause, p.82

3/Hack: As the name suggests, light is central to Illuminationism, used metaphorically to explore both the physical universe and a hidden, underlying reality that is the domain of the Light of Lights – or God, as Western thought normally puts it.

No.49
René Descartes' Evil Genius
Quintessential puppetmaster?

 1/ Helicopter view: René Descartes (1596–1650), who is often credited with being the Father of Modern Philosophy, contributed significantly to what has become known as the *Epistemological Turn*. This is the *turn away* from metaphysical investigations of things "out there" in reality and taking for granted that they exist as they appear to us, and the turn *toward* how it is we come to know anything with absolute certainty. (Note that *epistēmē* is the Greek word for "knowledge".) Descartes rejected the so-called reliability of sensation – for him, seeing is *not* believing. In his famous work, *Meditations on First Philosophy*, Descartes talks about how his senses deceive him time and time again – towers that looked round from a distance are actually square upon closer inspection, for example. But someone could argue that not *all* of our senses are deceiving us *all* the time. After all, the tower that was mistakenly thought to be round through the usage of sight was also *correctly identified* as square through the usage of sight.

This advertisement for the US magician (Harry) Kellar, from 1894, is a terrifying representation of the chaos of a world without certainty.

2/ Shortcut: To show it's possible that we could be wrong about all our sensations, as well as things that seem so absolutely certain to us, such as the so-called truths of logic – if A, then B; not B, so not A; mathematics (2+2=4); and natural laws (gravity, motion and causation) – Descartes posits that there could be an Evil Genius that is powerful enough to deceive us in a wholesale, systematic fashion, such that *everything* we think we know to be true or correct is *actually* false or incorrect. According to Descartes, however, there is one thing that the Evil Genius cannot deceive us about – but you'll have to read the entry on *René Descarte's Cogito* (see pages 104–5) to find that out…

See also //
33 Avicenna's Floating Man, p.70
50 René Descartes' *Cogito*, p.104
51 René Descartes' substance dualism, p.106

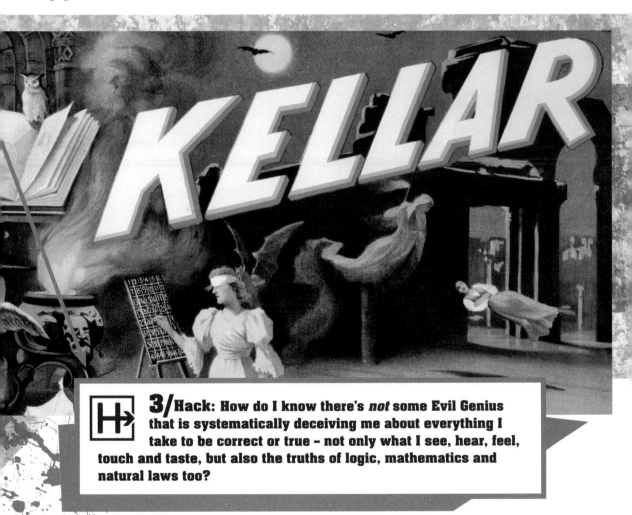

3/ Hack: How do I know there's *not* some Evil Genius that is systematically deceiving me about everything I take to be correct or true – not only what I see, hear, feel, touch and taste, but also the truths of logic, mathematics and natural laws too?

René Descartes' *Cogito*

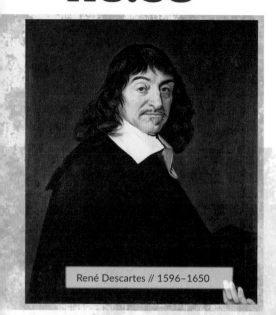

René Descartes // 1596–1650

Thinking requires an existing thinker

1/ Helicopter view: In his famous work *Meditations on First Philosophy*, René Descartes (1596–1650) posits that there could be an Evil Genius that is powerful enough to deceive us in a wholesale, systematic fashion, such that *everything* we think we know to be true or correct is actually false or incorrect. This includes sensations, as well as things that seem so absolutely certain to us, such as the so-called truths of logic: if A, then B; not B, so not A; mathematics (2+2=4); and natural laws (gravity, motion and causation). In the movie *The Truman Show,* think of the way Christof and his production team deceive Truman Burbank, or the way in which the Intelligent Machines deceive humanity (except for Morpheus and the rest of the crew of the *Nebuchadnezzar*) in the movie *The Matrix*. Now think of a being with enough power to make it such that we can never, ever know whether we are being deceived or not, at least not in the way Truman or Morpheus are able to uncover the deceptions they encounter. "But," Descartes says in the *Meditations*, "let him deceive me as much as he will, he can never cause me to be nothing so long as I think that I am something." Descartes argues that if he is thinking, he has to be existing, and even if there is some Evil Genius systematically deceiving him, this being cannot be systematically deceiving Descartes about one thing – namely, the fact that he exists, because he affirms that he exists every time he thinks!

Descartes' *Principles of Philosophy* was essentially an egotistical reissue of his earlier writings.

2/Shortcut: Even if Descartes is being deceived about everything else in life – for example, 2+2 *actually* = 5; up is *really* down (and vice-versa); and your body is an illusion or is not actually your own – there's one thing that the Evil Genius cannot deceive him about: *Je pense, donc je suis* (*Cogito, ergo sum*). If I'm thinking, claims Descartes, then there must be some *thing that is existing* to be doing the thinking in the first place – some thing that is "am"-ing. Otherwise, there would be no thinking and no thoughts occurring. So, if I think, I am (existing to be able to do the thinking). I think. Therefore, I am.

See also //

49 René Descartes' Evil Genius, p.102

51 René Descartes' substance dualism, p.106

3/Hack: I think, therefore I am, *Je pense, donc je suis. Cogito, ergo sum.*

No.51
René Descartes' substance dualism
Mind over matter

1/Helicopter view: Most of us have heard the famous dictum of René Descartes (1596–1650) – "I think, therefore I am" – at some point in our lives. This simple argument was put forward in response to a thought experiment that Descartes considered in his famous work, *Meditations on First Philosophy*. The thought experiment concerns the possibility of the existence of an Evil Genius that is powerful enough to deceive us in a wholesale, systematic fashion, such that *everything* we think we know to be true or correct is *actually* false or incorrect. Descartes argues that there's one thing that this Evil Genius cannot deceive him about, namely that he is existing, as long as he is thinking – hence, the birth of the "I think, therefore I am" argument. However, immediately afterward, Descartes considers the nature of the "thing that exists" doing the thinking. What is it exactly? He thinks it is *l'âme* ("the soul"), which for him would have been the same thing as the mind. And he believes that his essential nature – what he is at his core – is a mind, a thinking thing, a substance existing in its own right that is different/distinct from anything else in reality, including the very body (a material thing) to which it would seem to be intimately connected.

One of Descartes' scientific diagrams intended to illustrate the theory of vision (above) and René Descartes himself (left).

2/ Shortcut: Nearly everyone on the planet thinks not only that the typical human has a mind and a body, but also that the mind is something very different from the body. The contemporary argument for the *complete* distinction between mind and body – such that the mind and the body are two utterly different kinds of things or substances – can actually be traced back to two arguments put forward by Descartes in his *Meditations*. We'll look at one of those here. It's an argument that can be gathered from parts of *Meditation I* and *II*, as well as *Meditation VI*:

Premise 1:	I cannot doubt the existence of my own mind.
Premise 2:	I can doubt the existence of my body.
Conclusion:	Therefore, my mind is something distinct from my body.

Magritte's painting *La Décalcomanie* (1966) explores the Surrealist principle of liberating thought, language and the human experience from reason (below).

See also //
16 Aesara of Lucania's tripartite soul, p.36
21 Aristotle's hylomorphism, p.46

3/ Hack: Since it is impossible to imagine ourselves not thinking (since to imagine something is itself a form of thinking) but possible to imagine that our bodies don't really exist, thought must have a different and higher kind of reality.

No.52

GODEFROI GUILLAUME
LEIBNITZ,
Né le 3 Juillet 1646 mort le 14 Novembre 1716.

Gottfried Wilhelm von Leibniz's pluralism

Building a universe out of mysterious monads

1/ Helicopter view: "I love Leibniz," said Voltaire, "He is surely a great genius, even if he is also a bit of a charlatan…add to that, his ideas are always a bit confused." Nowhere is this truer than with the pluralism of Gottfried Wilhelm von Leibniz (1646–1716). After all, his main idea is that everything in the universe consists of *just one thing*, which he called monads, while the essence of pluralism is that it is made up of many things. In addition, Leibniz's monads, although ill defined and eminently mysterious, are said to be fundamental, while pluralism insists that no one thing can be more fundamental than another.

Nonetheless, Leibniz allows his monads to vary and so, in the history of philosophy, his pluralism is still a contrast to the dualism of René Descartes (1596–1650; see pages 102–7) and the monism of Baruch Spinoza (1632–1677; see pages 110–11). Descartes divides the universe into mind and matter, while Spinoza sees the universe as being made of just one thing – a kind of god – and regards the appearance of diversity as an illusion. In *Monadology*, a work published in 1720, Leibniz writes:

"Every portion of matter can be thought of as a garden full of plants, or as a pond full of fish. But every branch of the plant, every part of the animal, and every drop of its vital fluids, is another such garden, or another such pool."

Leibniz uses the analogy of a choir singing in harmony (right) to explain the apparent inter-relationship of matter.

2/ Shortcut: In fact, pluralism, or the "doctrine of multiplicity", is generally taken as indicating that reality is fragmentary and indeterminate. Leibniz sees contradictions in the notion of atoms, empty space and time too. So, instead, he builds the universe up out of the monads. These are "simple substances without parts and without windows through which anything could come in or go out". They occupy no space, but are "extension-less".

The only difference Leibniz allows in order to distinguish one monad from another is energy, and the only activity monads partake in is perception. At the time Leibniz was writing, the word "perception" was used in a biological sense, so, for example, a plant might perceive the heat of the sun and turn toward it.

Leibniz divides his monads into various categories, "bare" monads that make up matter, souls and spirits. The superior monads, the spirits, are living atoms, conscious and able to imagine the future.

Monads cannot interact (which is why Leibniz says that they have "no windows"), but, nonetheless, the universe behaves as if they were all somehow linked. Leibniz thinks this can be explained by the monads all sharing a pre-established routine – he uses the analogy of a choir all singing from the same song sheet. Monads do not affect one another and yet each one expresses the entire universe.

See also //
21 Aristotle's hylomorphism, p.46
51 René Descartes' substance dualism, p.106

3/ Hack: Leibniz constructs the universe out of a vast number of mysterious objects that he calls monads, which have different properties and do not directly interact, but nonetheless are operating within an all-encompassing, pre-established harmony.

No.53
Baruch Spinoza's monism
Seeing everything as a harmonious whole

1/ Helicopter view: Baruch Spinoza (1632–1677) is a rather odd philosopher. He could have taken up a chair in Philosophy at Heidelberg University, in Germany, but preferred to spend his days in Amsterdam, polishing and grinding to make optical and scientific lenses. Mind you, lens grinding was better paid than university teaching in those days. This meant Spinoza could only write in his spare time and, as a result, he published just two books in his lifetime. The better known is *Ethics*, which sets out his argument for monism, but the first was *The Principles of Descartes' Philosophy*, with a foreword noting that he disagreed with most of it. Specifically, unlike René Descartes (1596–1650; see pages 102–7), Spinoza did not think there were two distinct things, mind and matter, but rather that both were but "aspects" of the same thing. For Spinoza, this "something" had many aspects, including that of being rocks, being animals and, above all, being God. Spinoza argued that the whole of the natural world, including human beings, follows one and the same set of natural laws. By implication, there is nothing – no immortal soul, for example – to make humans special.

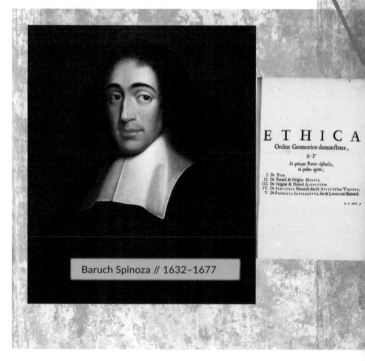

Baruch Spinoza // 1632–1677

ETHICA
Ordine Geometrico demonstrata ,

Spinoza's God is a funny sort of god that might be better thought of as "nature", and certainly can't be separated from it. "Except God, no substance can be or be conceived," he wrote. And since God exists necessarily, so does everything in the universe.

An 18th-century illustration (right) of Spinoza, walking with a book in hand in Amsterdam, spurned by the local Jewish community.

2/Shortcut: So radical is Spinoza's monism that he says each individual entity, that is you and me, tables and chairs, dogs and cats, is in reality only one part of the whole —"localized concentrations of the attributes of one greater reality", to use philosophical jargon. The proof of this is that a vast causal chain links everything, in the process making things such as "free will" purely illusory. Spinoza earnestly insists that things we imagine to be "evil" are perfectly acceptable when seen as part of this overall picture – or seen "from the perspective of eternity", as he puts it.

See also //

21 Aristotle's hylomorphism, p.46
51 René Descartes' substance dualism, p.106

3/Hack: Spinoza's theory of the structure of the universe is known as substance monism: within it, there is only one infinite substance – God – but this exists in many forms.

No.54
John Locke's *tabula rasa*
Where do our ideas come from?

1/ Helicopter view: The English philosopher John Locke (1632–1704) popularized the concept that the human mind begins at birth as a *tabula rasa* (or "blank slate"), devoid of content until etched with knowledge through life's experiences. Locke even described the human mind as "white paper, void of all characters". While Locke did acknowledge limited innate awareness, he characterized this as both "trifling" and empty of content. The debate has profound implications in relation to the branch of philosophy called epistemology (see page 44), which is concerned with what we know and believe, and how knowledge is derived through experience and reasoning.

Contrary to Locke's assumption, modern scientists now think that the human brain is preprogrammed to make sense of information in sophisticated ways.

2/Shortcut: Although it was John Locke who made famous the analogy of the human mind being a virtual blank slate at the moment of birth, he was not the first or last philosopher to discuss the broad issue. For example, Aristotle (384–322 BCE; see pages 46–53) and the Stoics (see pages 54–5) held similar views two millennia earlier, as did David Hume (1711–1776; see pages 116–19) two centuries later. Even today, the issue continues to be right at the heart of the science of the mind, which is providing us with an increasingly important alternative window onto how the human mind works. In particular, science has demonstrated that, through genetics, the brain has already developed specialized functions that influence thoughts and behaviours before a baby enters the world.

See also //
20 Knowledge, p.44
77 Perceiver, perception and perceived, p.158

John Locke // 1632-1704

Contrary to Locke's model of a *tabula rasa* ("blank slate"), this preprogramming, which is enriched by the mind's malleability, shapes human cognition, endowing the human newborn with the ability to think and learn in increasingly sophisticated ways: acquiring language, performing calculations, identifying objects, analysing surroundings, reasoning and building coherent ideas, and navigating spatially.

3/Hack: While it is true that the bulk of learning obviously comes both empirically and rationally after birth, practical research in recent years has shown that the brain possesses innate thoughts and abilities prior to birth, which contradicts Locke's blank-slate metaphor.

No.55
George Berkeley's *esse est percipi*
Putting mind over matter

1/Helicopter view: The Irish philosopher Bishop George Berkeley (1685–1753) is a much more subtle and important thinker than he is often given credit for. His doctrine that "to be is to be perceived" – or *esse est percipi* in the original Latin – is in many ways a synthesis of both Eastern and Western philosophy. But that is not to say, of course, that it is right. Indeed, Berkeley's ideas attracted much derision both at the time and since. Dr. Samuel Johnson (1709–1784), the famous writer and lexicographer, was supposed to have dismissed the notion that there are no material objects, only minds and ideas in those minds, by kicking a large stone and saying, "I refute it thus."

The number "42" on the Ishihara colour test plate below is visible to those with normal colour vision but, in a sense, does not exist for those who cannot see it.

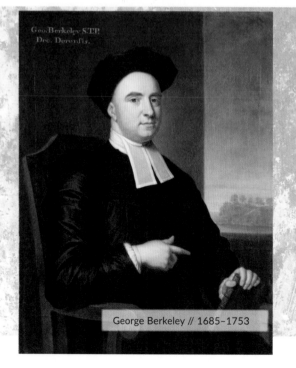

George Berkeley // 1685–1753

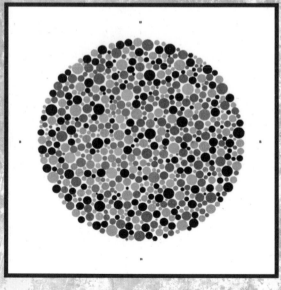

2/Shortcut: Berkeley produced his main writings in his twenties. His argument against matter is set out in *Dialogues of Hylas and Philonous* (1713), where it is presented as an exchange of views between the two characters, as if they were in a play. Hylas stands for the conventional, scientific view, while Philonous presents Berkeley's ideas. After an amiable preamble, Hylas challenges his friend to defend his belief that there is no such thing as matter. Can anything be more fantastical, more repugnant to commonsense than that, he exclaims!

Philonous responds that sense data are, in fact, mental, and illustrates the point by using lukewarm water as an example. To a cold hand, the water appears warm; to a hot hand, it appears cold. Hylas accepts this, but clings to other evidence of the material world derived from the senses. Philonous replies that tastes and smells are also mental judgements. Hylas counters this with the comment that sounds cannot travel through a vacuum, pointing out that this proves they must be motions of air molecules, not mental entities. Philonous responds that if this is indeed sound, then it bears no resemblance to what we perceive. Similar arguments are used to dismiss the objective reality of colours and size.

When Hylas argues that the act of perception may be mental, but that there is still a material object, Philonous insists that for something to be perceived, there must be a mind somewhere to perceive it.

See also //
20 Knowledge, p.44
77 Perceiver, perception and perceived, p.158

 3/Hack: Berkeley's point is that there are logical grounds for holding the view that only minds and mental events can exist.

No.56
Not all swans are white

And you can't be sure bread will nourish you

David Hume // 1711–1776

 1/ Helicopter view: David Hume (1711–1776; see also pages 118–19) was perhaps the greatest sceptic the Western world has ever produced, given that he was wholly unsure about the existence, reality or reliability of absolutely, positively, anything whatsoever. For example, you've let go of a ball a thousand times before, and it always falls to the ground. So, you reason, by something called *induction*: "Because I've seen the ball drop to the ground so many times before, I can conclude that this time it will drop to the floor when I let go of it." Or, you have observed many emeralds, and each has been green in appearance; therefore, you reason that all emeralds are green in appearance. Another example: you have observed many swans, and each has been white; therefore, you reason that all swans are white. However, when it comes to matters such as these, where we're dealing with facts and figures about the world, we could always be wrong. There is always the *possibility* that the next swan you observe will *not* be white, or that the next emerald you see will *not* be green, or even that the ball will hover in mid-air or go upward when you let go of it! Although there are no recorded instances of the last two examples, in 1790 John Latham (1740–1837), the English Father of Ornithology, did discover *black* swans in southeast and southwest regions of Australia. So, *not* all swans are white.

For many centuries it was assumed that there were no black swans (right). Their discovery in Australia in the 18th century came as a great surprise.

2/Shortcut: To highlight the impossibility of being completely sure of anything, David Hume uses the causal connection between bread's nourishing properties as a cause and the body's capacity to be nourished by bread (and other substances) as an effect. He points out that we never actually see the causal connection between the two. We never *see* bread *nourishing* the body; we just see bread "touch" the body at a certain time through the mouth and we see the body "being touched" by the bread at a later time.

See also //

20 Knowledge, p.44

77 Perceiver, perception and perceived, p.158

3/Hack: David Hume thinks we are wholly unsure about the existence, reality or reliability of absolutely, positively anything whatsoever, including whether that next piece of bread we eat will actually nourish us.

No.57
David Hume's compatibilism

Internally determined, yet externally free

1/Helicopter view: *Determinism* is the belief that all occurrences, circumstances and events – basically anything that has ever happened, including the choices that humans supposedly make of their own "free" will – are completely *determined* by previously existing causes. If you think of everything that has occurred since the Big Bang, there is a way of looking at all these potentially infinite interactions as *necessarily happening* to bring us to the point where we are today. Determinism is much harder to believe when it comes to human action and interaction with the world, because we think we have the freedom to create new causal chains, or even stop a causal chain. However, thinkers such as the Scottish philosopher David Hume (1711–1776; see also pages 116–17) have argued otherwise. According to Hume, the world around you determines your desires, which then determine your motivations, which then determine your intention (or will) to act on those motivations, which then determines the execution of your intention to act.

David Hume // 1711–1776

Statue of Scottish philosopher David Hume by sculptor Alexander Stoddart. Hume is dressed in the robes of an Ancient Greek philosopher (left).

2/ Shortcut: If you have no control over yourself, then how can you be held accountable or responsible for what you do or don't do? David Hume's response to this has been referred to as *compatibilism*. Hume thinks that while you are completely determined (that is, not "free") to act a certain way, you still need to have external "freedom of space or movement" in which to realize your actions. So, internal determinism and external "freedom" are made compatible with one another. The way to rehabilitate people, then, is to change a person's desires, which will then change motivations, change intentions and change actions. The trick is to get people to desire the right kinds of things.

A caged bird may have lost its freedom to fly but retains the limited right to sing (below).

See also //
58 Baron d'Holbach's metaphysical monism, p.120
81 Existential authenticity, p.166

3/ Hack: According to David Hume, we are internally determined to act in a certain way, but when there is nothing to prevent us from carrying out that act which is external to us, we are free; thus determinism and freedom (in a limited sense) are made compatible with one another.

Baron d'Holbach // 1723–1789

Baron d'Holbach's metaphysical monism

Materialism, mechanism, matter and motion

 1/ Helicopter view: There are a variety of beliefs about what exists "out there" in reality. There is *metaphysical monism*, the belief that only one "kind" of thing exists; but, this one thing could be a realm, a principle or a category, and it could have different modes (modalities, manifestations, facets). There are different types of monists too. There are immaterialists who believe that the one thing is really just immaterial (mental, mind, spiritual) and that the material physical things we see around us are an illusion, and there are materialists who believe that the one thing is material (physical, spatio-temporal) and that talk of the immaterial is just that – talk. There is also *metaphysical pluralism*, which is the belief that many kinds of things exist, of which *trialism* and *dualism* are the basic two kinds. Trialists believe in the material (for example, human bodies), the immaterial (for example, human souls) and something above or beyond both (for example, God in the Judeo-Islamic-Christian sense), while dualists believe in the material and the immaterial only. A good deal of the world's population subscribes to materialism. Why is that? The short answer has to do with advances that have been made in medicine and technology since the Scientific Revolution (see pages 94–5) of the 15th, 16th and 17th centuries. Paul-Henri Thiry (Baron) d'Holbach (1723–1789) was born in the wake of the Scientific Revolution and was one of the most outspoken advocates of materialism in Western history.

A late 19th-century engraving showing the machine room in the industrialist Richard Hartmann's factory in Chemnitz Germany (right).

2/Shortcut: In Baron d'Holbach's famous work *System of Nature*, he notes simply and succinctly: "The universe, that vast assemblage of every thing that exists, presents only matter and motion: the whole offers to our contemplation nothing but an immense, an uninterrupted succession of causes and effects." Holbach's metaphysics, then, is wholly materialistic and mechanistic, in that any correct explanation of an event will refer only to matter, motion and the laws that describe their causal connection.

See also //

45 Francis Bacon's gift to science, p.94

57 David Hume's compatibilism, p.118

3/Hack: Baron d'Holbach's metaphysics is completely materialistic and mechanistic, in that any correct explanation of a given event will only refer to matter, motion and the laws that describe their causal connection.

No.59
Immanuel Kant's transcendental idealism
A Copernican revolution in our way of thinking about reality

1/ Helicopter view: Immanuel Kant (1724–1804; see also pages 124–5) is one of the greatest philosophers of the Western world because he was able to synthesize the ideas of his predecessors so adroitly and use them as a springboard for his own theories. These have remained the bedrock for metaphysicians, epistemologists, ethicists and other thinkers to this day. Kant dealt with two main groups of thinkers: the Continental Rationalists (René Descartes, Baruch Spinoza, Gottfried Wilhelm von Leibniz) and the British Empiricists (John Locke, George Berkeley, David Hume). Whereas Empiricists held that all knowledge originated in – and is ultimately limited by – sense experience, the Rationalists mistrusted sense perception because it could be inaccurate at times. Instead, they believed that knowledge is founded upon clear, distinct, precise ideas that the mind discovers about reality. Kant was thrust into this tug of war between the two schools of thought, and came up with a genius plan: a Copernican Revolution in our way of thinking about thinking. Whereas Nicolaus Copernicus (1473–1543) decided to switch his perspective and consider himself as moving on the Earth while the Sun stood still (in contrast to the geocentricism of his time), Kant decided to switch his perspective and consider that the mind is active and adds something to the knowing process. This was in contrast to both the Rationalists and Empiricists, who believed the mind to be a kind of passive thing waiting to be *affected*.

Immanuel Kant // 1724–1804

Kant shown dining with friends in an 1892/3 painting by Emil Dörstling (above right).

2/Shortcut: The result of this "paradigm shift" in our way of thinking about thinking is known as Immanuel Kant's *transcendental idealism*. Space and time are the things we "add" to anything we experience in order to help us make sense of that experience. Furthermore, all we ever know are the things that we can experience, as they *appear* to us – we can never know about those things as they are in and of themselves.

See also //

20 Knowledge, p.44

77 Perceiver, perception and perceived, p.158

3/Hack: Immanuel Kant offers the best and simplest explanation of transcendental idealism: "By transcendental idealism I mean that appearances are to be regarded as representations only, not things in themselves, and that time and space are therefore only sensible forms of our intuition."

No.60

Immanuel Kant's moral theory

Actions that are right or wrong, categorically speaking

IMMANUEL KANT
From a painting

1/ Helicopter view: Most people know that it's wrong to do certain things like rape, murder, exploit people, cheat on taxes and shoplift. When we begin articulating the moral principles that act as the justification or grounding for why these actions are wrong, then we are trading in the realm of *ethics* or *moral philosophy*. The moral philosophy of Immanuel Kant (1724–1804; see also pages 122–3) sets him apart as the foremost proponent of *deontology* – *deontos* is Greek for "duty" – with what he calls the *categorical imperative*. The *categorical* part means there is only one absolute, apodictic (that is, clearly established) set of rules; the *imperative* part entails the duty to act (a prescriptivity, an ought, a should).

Kant has three formulations of the categorical imperative, two of which we talk about here. The first is: whenever you act, make sure your action is something that can be universalized without contradiction. In other words, ask yourself the question, "What if everyone did what I'm about to do?" If the answer undermines or negates what you want to do, then it's immoral and you should not do it! For example, if you wanted to borrow money without paying it back and imagined a world where all people did this, then the idea of "borrowing" would cease to exist, and you would have nothing to borrow in the first place – hence, generating this contradiction, undermining your initial desire, and making your action wrong.

The categorical imperative is a moral law that is binding on everyone – by virtue of its own binding logic.

2/ Shortcut: The second of the three formulations of Immanuel Kant's categorical imperative is: whenever you act, always treat yourself and others with respect by never using yourself or others as a means to an end. In other words, don't ever objectify or exploit yourself or another person for any reason whatsoever, no matter what the circumstances. Makes sense, doesn't it?

See also //
68 Good for the majority, p.140
88 John Rawls' original position, p.180

3/ Hack: Whenever you act, always treat yourself and others with respect by never using yourself or others as a means to an end.

William Paley's watchmaker analogy

Human designs watch, God designs universe

William Paley // 1743–1805

1/ Helicopter view: There are really two types of reasoning. The first is where we think that some claim follows necessarily from some other claim(s). This is called *deductive reasoning*, as in, "Bachelors are unmarried males and Frank is a bachelor, so *Frank is definitely an unmarried male.*" The other is where we think that some claim probably follows from some other claim(s). This is called inductive reasoning, as in, "Most Republicans are conservative and Mary is a Republican, so *Mary is likely/probably a conservative.*" In the deductive realm of reasoning, there are many types of deductive arguments; the one above about Frank is an example of *universal instantiation*. There are also many types of inductive arguments, a popular one we use all the time being an *argument from analogy*. In this argument, one compares two things that are relevantly similar and, given the similarity, reasons that the same qualities, attributes or circumstances in the one will also likely/probably be found in the other. Many thinkers have used an argument from analogy in an attempt to prove the existence of a god, one of them being William Paley (1743–1805), an English philosopher and clergyman whose watchmaker analogy is, well, timeless…

Darwin himself commented on Paley's writings: "The logic of this book and, as I may add, of his *Natural Theology*, gave me as much delight as did Euclid."

2/Shortcut: William Paley's argument is elegantly simple: if you are walking in a forest and find a watch, would you think that it must have had a watchmaker, by virtue of it having complex parts that are hierarchically organized and all working together for the common goal of telling the time. So, too, Paley argues, if you look around the universe at things such as the eye, or other biological entities, or even the seasons of the year, it is likely that the universe has a universe-Maker – what we call God.

See also //

37 Ultimate cause of everything, p.78

91 Richard Dawkins' blind watchmaker, p.186

3/Hack: In the same way that a watch is complex, organized and goal-directed, and has a maker, so, too, is the universe complex, organized and goal-directed; therefore, it is likely that the universe has a maker as well – God.

No.62
Adam Smith's hidden hand
Letting market-forces do their work

1/Helicopter view: Scotland's Adam Smith (1813–1893) was a radical thinker. Where earlier philosophers, such as Plato (428–348 BCE; see pages 40–5) and John Locke (1632–1704; see pages 112–13), believed that society needed to be based on altruism, or at least the suppression of selfishness – as in Niccolò Machiavelli (1469–1527; see pages 92–3) and Thomas Hobbes (1588–1679; see pages 96–7) – Smith inverted the natural order and made self-interest the key to making the world go round. Rather than call on wise guardians and human goodness (backed by strict public codes), Smith allows society to be ordered by an entirely greater force: economics. Nonetheless, Smith is concerned not only with money, but also with justice and equity.

In *An Inquiry into the Nature and Causes of The Wealth of Nations*, published in 1766, Smith explains that: "...every individual necessarily labours to render the annual revenue of the society as great as he can. He generally, indeed, neither intends to promote the public intent, nor knows how much he is promoting it... he intends only his own gain, and he is in this, as in many other cases, led by an invisible hand to promote an end which was no part of his intention."

This is the original expression of the theory generally known as the "Invisible Hand", or the "Hidden Hand", although Smith never actually used that phrase. It's a powerful idea, which suggests that there is a character and reality to social action over and above the intentions of the individuals that make up societies.

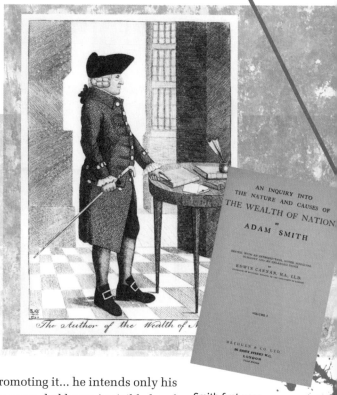

The Author of the Wealth of N[ations]

AN INQUIRY INTO
THE NATURE AND CAUSES OF
THE WEALTH OF NATIONS
ADAM SMITH

EDITED WITH AN INTRODUCTION, NOTES MARGINAL SUMMARY AND AN ENLARGED INDEX

EDWIN CANNAN, M.A., LL.D.

VOLUME I

METHUEN & CO. LTD.
LONDON

Smith first uses the "Invisible Hand" metaphor in his book *The Theory of Moral Sentiments* (1759), where he insists that the rich are obliged to share their wealth with others.

2/Shortcut: In a much-quoted phrase from *The Wealth of Nations*, Adam Smith says that it is not out of the benevolence of the butcher or the baker that we can expect our supper; it is from their enlightened notion of their own self-interest. Smith's critics pointed out that individual desire for short-term personal gain could sometimes be at odds with the collective and national interest, and that, in the process, all might lose. Yet Smith's *laissez-faire* ("let it be") approach has the great advantage of co-opting individual enterprise and initiative, whereas such things are suppressed within command economies.

See also //

69 Karl Marx's *Communist Manifesto*, p.142

88 John Rawls' original position, p.180

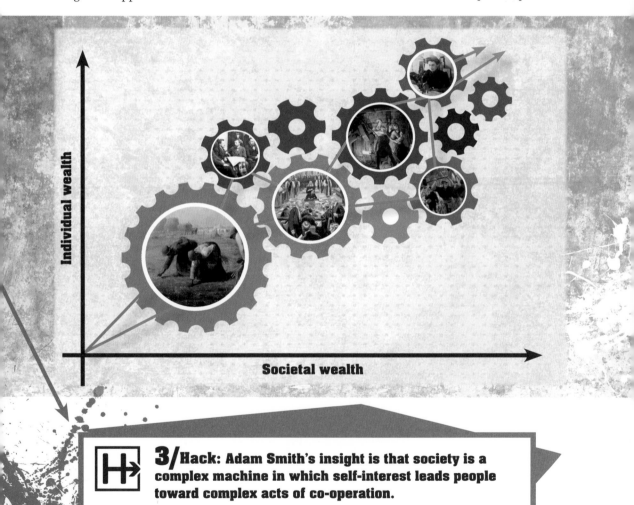

Individual wealth

Societal wealth

3/Hack: Adam Smith's insight is that society is a complex machine in which self-interest leads people toward complex acts of co-operation.

No.63
Johann G Fichte's Thesis-Antithesis-Synthesis process

How the mind resolves its own contradictions

Johann G Fichte // 1762–1814

1/Helicopter view: The Thesis-Antithesis-Synthesis process, or *dialectic*, as it is more normally called, has a long history. Its roots are in Eastern notions of yin and yang (see pages 16–17), but it also underlies the philosophy of Plato (428–348 BCE; see pages 40–5) and features within Immanuel Kant (1724–1804; see pages 122–5) in the form of four *antinomies*, or contradictions.

For Socrates (470–399 BCE; see pages 38–9) and Plato, the dialectic was a process by which the mind could proceed in the search for truth. However, for Georg Wilhelm Friedrich Hegel (1770–1831; see pages 132–3) and the later Marxists, the dialectic was also supposed to reflect the practical reality of world history and nature, as played out in the form of violent social conflicts and revolutions. In this way, it moved from being a mental feature within to a tangible physical phenomenon without.

Kant is content to note that reflection on any one aspect of the world often leads to a contemplation of its opposite, and it was left to Hegel to stress that the contradiction can be united by a shift to some higher level of thought. It is possible that Hegel was influenced in this by a passage from *The Science of Knowledge* by Johann Gottlieb Fichte (1762–1814), in which he offers a very particular example of the approach in relation to individual conscious-nesses.

Fichte's role in developing dialectical reasoning can be overstated, but his insights into subjectivity and consciousness are increasingly appreciated.

2/Shortcut: Fichte makes use of the Thesis-Antithesis-Synthesis approach in describing the confrontation between the Ego and the non-Ego (by which he means everything else, or the world). This has no real separate existence, but merely results from the Ego's self-conscious reflection. Fichte modifies Kant's approach, which had previously split reality into what we think we see (*phenomena*) and an underlying reality that is forever out of reach (*noumena*), by saying that there is only one world of mental constructs. Writing at about the same time, Arthur Schopenhauer (1788–1860; see pages 134–5) would have none of this, accusing Fichte of having "appealed boldly and openly to intellectual intuition, that is, really to inspiration". (See below for full quotation.)

See also //

1 Hinduism's theism, p.6

2 Saṃsāra, p.8

64 Georg Wilhelm Friedrich Hegel's Absolute Spirit, p.132

"Fichte who, because the thing-in-itself had just been discredited, at once prepared a system without any thing-in-itself...For this purpose, he...declared everything to be a priori, naturally without any evidence for such a monstrous assertion; instead of these, he gave sophisms and even crazy sham demonstrations whose absurdity was concealed under the mask of profundity and of the incomprehensibility ostensibly arising therefrom. Moreover, he appealed boldly and openly to intellectual intuition, that is, really to inspiration."

Arthur Schopenhauer, *Parerga and Paralipomena*

3/Hack: Fichte argues that the contradiction between the self and the world (or the "not-self"/non-Ego) can be resolved only by creating a third concept that unites the two. This he calls "the concept of divisibility" and it is produced by "discovering in opposites the respect in which they are alike".

No.64

Georg Wilhelm Friedrich Hegel // 1770–1831

Georg Wilhelm Friedrich Hegel's Absolute Spirit

A very austere God

1/Helicopter view: The first and most celebrated work of Georg Wilhelm Friedrich Hegel (1770–1831) is *The Phenomenology of Spirit* (or *Mind*). During his lifetime, Hegel published many other works and his political ideas led to the "historical materialism" of Karl Marx (1818–1883; see pages 142–3), as well as to the development of fascist ideology in Italy. Lying behind his totalitarian concept of society was a view of the universe, not as a collection of fundamental particles, whether atoms or souls, but as a whole, an organic unity. "The True is the Whole", Hegel explains. It is an illusion to think of anything as being separate from anything else, and, in as much as we do so, our thinking is flawed. The whole is also "The Absolute" and is rather like God.

The notion of an Absolute Spirit, free from any limitations – universal, unlimited, god-like, in effect – has been around for a long time. Hegel's schoolmate and fellow German, Friedrich Schelling, used it to signify a kind of epochal self-awareness, in which the knower becomes united with that which is known. But, for Hegel, this self-awareness was synonymous with truth and knowledge, and the final triumph of abstract logic. He predicted this as a (somewhat implausible) consequence of the evolution of human society. The term "spirit" really is a bit misleading, however; it might be better to think of it as "mind".

2/ Shortcut: Hegel says that the nature of the Absolute Spirit is the pursuit of self-aware rationality: logical thinking. He even seriously proposed that the Prussian state of his time represented the earthly manifestation of the Absolute Spirit, because he saw just the right sort of logic and rationality in the practical arrangements of the state.

Hegel argues that reality must be rational, and so its ultimate structure is revealed in the structure of our thought. In order to see how, Hegel offers philosophy as the way by which the Absolute gradually discovers and expresses its own grand nature, culminating in a synthesis of human culture. As Bertrand Russell (1872–1970; see pages 152–3) mocked, in this way Hegel makes his own thoughts the final and ultimate pinnacle of human development.

The March on Rome in 1922 resulted in Mussolini's National Fascist Party coming to power in Italy. The Italian fascists were inspired by Neo-Hegelian ideas.

See also //

1 Hinduism's theism, p.6
63 Johann G Fichte's Thesis-Antithesis-Synthesis process, p.130

3/ Hack: Hegel's notion of the Absolute Spirit turns the universe into a kind of machine for generating pure, logical truths.

No.65
Arthur Schopenhauer's
pessimism The poor consolation of philosophy

Arthur Schopenhauer // 1788–1860

1/ Helicopter view: "Life is a difficult question; I have decided to spend my life in thinking about it." Thus wrote Arthur Schopenhauer (1788–1860) in a letter to his friend, the poet Christoph Martin Wieland. Unlike many philosophers who are focused on anything but human needs and concerns, Schopenhauer is focused on finding a philosophy that is far more than mere words on a page, but a real tool for making sense of existence. In the process, he ends up embracing a view in which existence is denounced in order to escape its absurdity. His ideas are presented in sharp and sardonic style in his book, *The World as Will and Representation*, published in 1819. However, it is in an essay called (appropriately enough) "On the Emptiness of Existence" that he best sums up his reasons to be cheerless:

"That human life must be a kind of mistake is sufficiently clear from the fact that man is a compound of needs, which are difficult to satisfy; moreover, if they are satisfied, all he is granted is a state of painlessness, in which he can only give himself up to boredom. This is a precise proof that existence in itself has no value."

In Greek mythology, Sisyphus (right) was condemned in perpetuity to the futile task of carrying a rock up a hill, which would then roll back down.

2/Shortcut: Central to Arthur Schopenhauer's philosophical system is the concept of "Will". This is what Freud would later adopt as a kind of hidden psychological master. Within Schopenhauer, it is something mindless, aimless and non-rational. The force traps humanity in continuous struggle and striving that are ultimately for nothing. Life, in general, has but one intrinsic aim, which is to reproduce and keep the species going – but there is no purpose within that. Schopenhauer sees people as automaton-like, with no greater horizon than that of attending to the practical needs of everyday existence. He warns gloomily that "the purpose of our existence is not to be happy" and that, logically, non-existence is preferable to existence. The only gleam of light that Schopenhauer can see in the dark picture that he paints is to "transcend" the everyday through what he calls "Aesthetic Perception". In such activity, our attention is distracted toward things that possess a more universal quality.

See also //

2 Saṃsāra, p.8

80 Existential nihilism, p.164

3/Hack: Arthur Schopenhauer regards human striving as insatiable, and any gratification from achieving a goal only momentary, soon turning back toward suffering.

No.66

Mary Wollstonecraft's vindication

An early feminist pamphlet

Mary Wollstonecraft // 1757–1797

A
VINDICATION
OF THE
RIGHTS OF WOMAN:
WITH
STRICTURES
ON
POLITICAL AND MORAL SUBJECTS.

BY MARY WOLLSTONECRAFT.

PRINTED AT BOSTON,
BY PETER EDES FOR THOMAS AND ANDREWS,
FAUST's Statue, No. 45, Newbury-Street,
MDCCXCII.

1/Helicopter view:
Mary Wollstonecraft (1757–1797) was one of the first overtly feminist philosophers. Writing in England, where she lived with her husband, the anarchist philosopher William Godwin (1756–1836), she offered a radical personal narrative, uncritically endorsing the politics of the French Revolution, even as some of her immediate circle were being led to the guillotine in France. Her book, *A Vindication of the Rights of Woman* (1792), pushed forward the liberal hypothesis of John Locke (1632–1704; see pages 112–13) on the political importance of women, with a wide-ranging denunciation of "male rationality" and power that targeted Edmund Burke (1729–1797) and Jean-Jacques Rousseau (1712–1778), in particular. For her outspoken advocacy of women's rights, Wollstonecraft earned the dislike of many prominent male intellectuals of the time, and the sobriquet of a "hyena in petticoats" from Horace Walpole (1717–1797).

Feminists count Wollstonecraft as the "first suffragette". She saw marriage as slavery and demanded equal rights for women explaining, "I do not wish [women] to have power over men, but over themselves."

2/ Shortcut: *A Vindication of the Rights of Woman* was written in 1791 and published in 1792. It was supposed to be Volume 1 of a larger work, but Wollstonecraft never wrote the subsequent parts. As such, it focuses on education in particular. In his book *Émile*, Rousseau had also argued for the reform of female education, partly for moral reasons, but mostly to better prepare women for an assumed future role as companions for men. In contrast, Wollstonecraft complains that:

See also //

84 Feminist philosophy, p.172

92 Simone de Beauvoir's *Second Sex*, p.188

"...the civilized women of this present century, with a few exceptions, are only anxious to inspire love, when they ought to cherish a nobler ambition, and by their abilities and virtues exact respect."

In fact, Wollstonecraft is less radical than her followers today might imagine. She borrows ideas from Rousseau's style of "philosophical anthropology" – that is, looking for philosophical insights by examining the behaviour of past and present societies – as well as political arguments that were made by John Locke, notably those advocating equal rights for women. The title of the book is itself a reference to another thinker's writings, in this case *A Vindication of the Rights of Man* by the political campaigner Thomas Paine (1737–1809), who was one of Wollstonecraft's contemporaries.

Jean-Jacques Rousseau // 1712–1778

3/ Hack: Wollstonecraft's central argument is that relations between men and women are corrupted by artificial notions of gender, just as relations between men and other men can be by notions of rank, wealth or heredity.

No.67

Auguste Comte's positivism
All hail the mighty scientific explanation

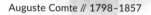
Auguste Comte // 1798–1857

1/Helicopter view: Auguste Comte (1798–1857) was a French thinker who coined the term *sociologie* to refer to *létude scientifique de l'homme* (or "the scientific study of human beings"). He was not only an atheist, but an anti-theist, a fervent supporter of naturalism (reality is comprised of natural properties and causes that are explainable through physical, chemical and biological laws of matter and motion, and supernatural or spiritual explanations are excluded or discounted); secular humanism (humanity is capable of achieving ideals of meaning, morality and, in general, all things beneficially superlative, on its own without any crutch of the divine); and scientism (the idea that the methodology and general world view of the scientist can be applied wholesale across all disciplines and life endeavours as *the* key to unlocking any door of the unexplained).

Comte envisioned the history of human knowledge – and all the sociological outgrowths from that knowledge – as having moved through three phases. The first phase he termed the Theological Phase, an infantile state in which humans blindly believe in some divine being, and society is ruled by shamans or by shamans who have the ear of kings and queens. Comte believed all primitive societies went through some period in which life is completely theocentric. From there, societies moved on to the Metaphysical Phase, which did not have the typical philosophical connotation of the word metaphysical – that is, referring to the "study of being" (see page 76) – but rather involved the justification of universal rights as existing on a higher plane than the authority of any god or shaman or human ruler speaking in the name of some god.

Scientists at the UK atomic research establishment at Harwell in 1957 (right). Comte dreamed of a world in which scientific explanations would dominate in all areas of human life.

2/Shortcut: Comte believed that the history of human knowledge had moved through three phases. The Theological Phase and Metaphysical Phase led to the third phase, which he referred to as the Scientific, or Positive, Phase, where scientific explanation is championed as applicable in all areas of human life and social interaction, and universal rights are abandoned in favour of *individual rights*. Interestingly enough, Comte thought that, in this final phase, all search for absolute knowledge is abandoned. This might appear counterintuitive to a modern-day scientist who knows that any scientific answer is always tentative, with more questions frequently being raised once answers have been revealed, so causing one to keep searching for what appears to be absolute knowledge.

See also //
45 Francis Bacon's gift to science, p.94
58 Baron d'Holbach's metaphysical monism, p.120

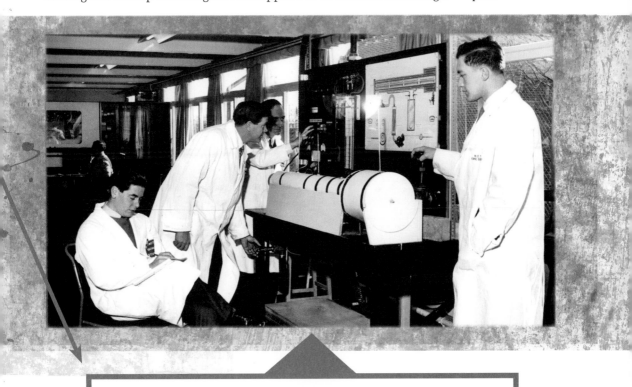

3/Hack: Comte's positivism champions scientific explanation as applicable in all areas of human life and social interaction, and universal rights are abandoned in favour of individual rights.

No.68
Good for the majority
Weighing the pros and cons with the utilitarian calculus

1/Helicopter view: When the United States dropped atomic bombs on the Japanese cities of Hiroshima and Nagasaki in 1945, many argued that, if they had not, the Japanese would have killed more Americans, more of their own people and more people from other countries, which would have caused the Second World War to rage on longer and longer – all of which would have been bad consequences, obviously. Conversely, although killing a couple of hundred thousand Japanese and destroying those cities was bad (obviously, a horrible, horrible thing), it was *not as bad* (in terms of consequences), given the aforementioned alternatives and what the Japanese had been doing during the war already, including the bombing of Pearl Harbor. Thus, many have argued that the US was justified in making the moral decision to drop the atomic bombs – again, based upon added-up, and adding up, harm and consequences. This is an incredibly controversial debate to this day, no doubt.

When you make moral/ethical decisions based on the *consequences* that are likely to occur, then you are considered a consequentialist, of which there are two kinds. One kind will act if, and only if, the consequences are beneficial to him/her – we call that person an *egoist*. The other kind makes a decision based on whether the consequences are going to benefit the majority of people affected by the decision – if the consequences are beneficial to the majority, he/she will act; if they're not, he/she won't act. That person we call a *utilitarian*. Many have argued that the US bombing of the Japanese cities of Hiroshima and Nagasaki in 1945 was a utilitarian decision.

John Stuart Mill // 1806–1873

Although utilitarian arguments were made for bombing Japan in 1945 (right), the Japanese were already seeking terms for surrender and the targets had no military significance.

2/ Shortcut: John Stuart Mill (1806–1873) is the philosopher most clearly associated with utilitarianism. The way in which the utilitarian determines the good consequences to all affected in a situation is through a pro versus con kind of calculus, or adding up all the benefits on one side and comparing them with all the detriments on the other side. The moral decision, then, is the one where the most benefits will result for the most people, and that's the one the utilitarian chooses.

See also //

46 Hobbes' *Leviathan*, p.96
88 John Rawls' original position, p.180

3/ Hack: The utilitarian principle: act only when the majority of the people affected by the action will gain some kind of benefit.

No.69
Karl Marx's *Communist Manifesto* Philosophy in action

Karl Marx // 1818–1883

Friedrich Engels // 1820–1895

1/ Helicopter view: Karl Heinrich Marx (1818–1883) was born and studied in Germany, becoming enthralled by philosophy and history, and the "dialectical" method of Georg Wilhelm Friedrich Hegel (1770–1831; see pages 132–3) in particular. This is the general theory in which everything inevitably generates its opposite, followed by a conflict from which a "synthesis" eventually emerges. However, Marx, along with his lifelong collaborator, the businessman Friedrich Engels (1820–1895), applied the method to economic life, creating what became known as "dialectical materialism". It is this idea, of economic classes locked in conflict, which is at the heart of *The Communist Manifesto*, a short and lively pamphlet written in 1848, the year known to historians as the Year of Revolutions.

The Communist Manifesto (right) is unusual within Marxist philosophy by being short and pithy. But, as Engels once remarked, "An ounce of action is worth a ton of theory."

2/ Shortcut: The *Manifesto* opens with the famous promise: "Let the ruling classes tremble at a communistic revolution. The proletarians have nothing to lose but their chains. They have a world to win!" It then offers in convenient summary form a list of the key ingredients for the revolution, including:

- Abolition of land ownership and rents
- A heavy progressive income tax and abolition of all inheritance rights
- Centralization of all capital and credit in a state bank
- State production through factories and farming, with "equal liability of all to labour"

Marx wanted the *Manifesto* to be the spark that would set fire to the rotten structures of European society, those by which a tiny elite of property-owning aristocrats exploited the labour of the masses. And the *Manifesto* not only predicts, but also describes, European society as already increasingly "splitting up into two great hostile camps, into two great classes directly facing each other: bourgeoisie and proletariat".

The "fundamental proposition" of the *Manifesto* is that "in every historical epoch" the prevailing "mode of economic production and exchange", and the social organization that necessarily follows from it, determines the political structures of society, along with the prevailing climate of intellectual beliefs and ideas.

Together, Marx and Engels produced many works that invariably offered a turgid mix of obscure philosophical theories and equally obscure economic factoids. However, it is the short and colourful *Manifesto* that left their mark on history.

See also //
46 Hobbes' *Leviathan*, p.96
62 Adam Smith's hidden hand, p.128

3/ Hack: The "whole history of mankind has been a history of class struggles, contests between exploiting and exploited, ruling and oppressed," denounces the *Manifesto* in one of its most memorable phrases.

The Kyoto School and nothingness

Going back to basics

Nishida Kitarō // 1870–1945

1/ Helicopter view: The Kyoto School is a group of 20th-century Japanese thinkers associated with Kyoto University, in Japan, who sought to develop a distinctively Eastern philosophy that drew on the intellectual and spiritual traditions of East Asia – notably those of Mahāyāna Buddhism in particular – as well as those of Western philosophy. The central figure of the Kyoto School is Nishida Kitarō (1870–1945), but the school should be properly understood as a group of thinkers involved in a cooperative and sustained attempt to develop a new philosophy rooted in the idea of "nothingness" or *zettai-mu* ("absolute nothingness"). This distinguishes their thought from that of traditional Western philosophies that focus on the concept of "being".

Nietzsche (right), seen here adopting a self-conscious Napoleonic pose, equates "nothingness" with "meaninglessness" but Eastern thinkers counted it as an alternative reality.

2/Shortcut: Although it aimed to create a distinctively Eastern philosophy, the Kyoto School actually mixes the traditional and Zen philosophies with elements of Western philosophy, notably the writings of Martin Heidegger (1889–1976; see pages 162–3), and Friedrich Nietzsche (1844–1900; see pages 148–9), who both make nothingness central to their writings. Indeed, Heidegger prefigures the Kyoto School by referring to *das Nichts* ("the nothing") as the "veil of being". And, in fact, Heidegger is himself revisiting older Western ideas, notably those of Georg Wilhelm Friedrich Hegel (1770–1831; see pages 132–3), which, in turn, link back to Ancient Greek ideas that have their own roots in the East. All of which explains why the Kyoto School thinkers generally consider the *purest* sources for the idea of absolute nothingness to lie in Eastern writings, which may be from India or China as well as Japan.

See also //
80 Existential nihilism, p.164
81 Existential authenticity, p.166

Where "being" is associated with a search for objective truth in the West, "nothingness" is linked with a kind of "transcendental subjectivity" of "the heart-mind" in the East. And, just as "being" in the West is associated with the "Supreme Being", or God, so nothingness for the Kyoto school requires an embrace of nihilism and a joining with Nietzsche in announcing the death of God.

3/Hack: Where Western philosophers focused on the search for "being" as the central aspect of the universe, the Kyoto School believed "nothingness" to be far more fundamental.

No.71
Søren Kierkegaard's leap of faith
A desperate remedy for doubt

1/Helicopter view: Søren Kierkegaard (1813–1855) was born in Copenhagen, Denmark, where he studied philosophy, theology and literature, but he also attended Berlin University during the 1840s while Friedrich Schelling (1775–1854) was lecturing there. He was inspired by Schelling's idea that philosophy begins with concepts and logical reasoning, but needs to switch to a deeper kind of thinking, which starts by saying that it is ultimately only the fact of existence that matters. In *Repetition*, published in 1843, Kierkegaard wrote, "I stick my finger in existence – it smells of nothing. Where am I? Who am I? How came I here? What is this thing called the world? What does this world mean? Who is it that has lured me into the world? Why was I not consulted…"

In *The Concept of Anxiety* (published a year later in 1844), Kierkegaard argues that all philosophical systems are empty because they do not equip one to face the reality of existence. The passions of the soul were important to Kierkegaard. His next step was to deny that there was such a thing as objective truth.

Søren Kierkegaard // 1813–1855

After this, as one contemporary commentator, Colin Kirk, has put it, the only possible way forward is to realize that it is imperative to live by your own truth, your own subjective truth. A leap of faith, a leap in the dark, is required, in which the thinker dares to break away from the protection of shared ideas – now seen as both a protective shared bond and a kind of prison.

For Kierkegaard, a leap in the dark is required, away from the protection of shared ideas, toward whatever is essential and vibrant in existence.

2/ Shortcut: Kierkegaard's "leap" harks back to the esoteric doctrines, not only of Ancient Greece, but also to the overtly mystical philosophers of the Far East. It also prefigures later themes of the existentialists (see pages 166–7 and 188–9). Although the phrase "leap of faith" is commonly attributed to Kierkegaard, he never uses the term as such. The nearest that he comes to it is in *Concluding Unscientific Postscript*, a book published in 1846, in which he describes the preliminary stage to the leap of faith as the kind of thinking that can turn toward itself in order to contemplate itself and give scepticism space to emerge. However, he warns, "this thinking about itself never accomplishes anything". Instead, he says that thinking should serve by thinking *something*, by embracing belief. It is this stepping away from bottomless self-reflection in favour of faith that constitutes the leap.

See also //

36 The greatest being conceivable, p.76

87 Alvin Plantinga's basic beliefs, p.178

THE JOURNALS OF SØREN KIERKEGAARD

A SELECTION EDITED AND TRANSLATED BY ALEXANDER DRU

UNIVERSITY PRESS
NEW YORK · TORONTO
1938

3/ Hack: Kierkegaard's "leap of faith" invites humanity to launch itself into the unknown and find itself in the process.

Friedrich Nietzsche's Overman
Beyond good and evil

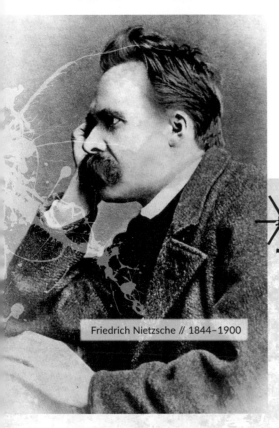

Friedrich Nietzsche // 1844–1900

1/Helicopter view: As well as being a philosopher, the German Friedrich Nietzsche (1844–1900) was also a historian with an interesting outlook on humanity and morality. With respect to humanity, he thought that people were selfish, pleasure-seeking animals who exerted their "will to power" over each other whenever they could. Obviously influenced by Charles Darwin's evolutionary theory of the survival of the fittest, Nietzsche posited that certain humans throughout history rose above *Die Herde* to become *Übermenschen* – literally, "Overmen". The Overman is not subject to the norms, customs, morays, rules or laws of the society in which he/she resides. In fact, the Overman tries to overpower and subjugate the herd whenever he/she can so that he/she can *make* the rules. "Might makes right" is certainly the mantra here. But it goes further than this: the Overman is *also* not subject to the *morality* of the herd who speak of good and evil in terms of justice, righteousness and equality. Such a morality is that of the *slave*. Nietzsche surveyed the various cultures throughout the history of the West, the East and the Middle East, and he noted that what each had in common was the fact that the standard moral laws laid down in, say, the Ten Commandments – for example, Thou shalt not covet, kill, steal, commit adultery – are derived from people who have become conquered, who are weak or powerless slaves. Morality favours mediocrity; standing beyond good and evil is to rise above the herd.

Nietzsche's Overman is sometimes called a superman but he is quite the opposite of the crimefighter of modern culture; instead he is above the law. Seen here (right) is Christopher Reeve from the renowned *Superman* film of 1978.

2/ Shortcut: The Overman is *Jenseits von Gut und Böse* ("Beyond Good and Evil") in *making* morality. He/she is a god among mere mortals, in this sense. The history of morals is the conflict of these two moral outlooks. The higher Overman is master and ruler, and creates his/her own values out of power, strength and domination; the lower herd is made up of slaves, ruled, meek, powerless and pathetic beings, who essentially hope to "kill the king with kindness".

See also //
80 Existential nihilism, p.164
81 Existential authenticity, p.166

3/ Hack: The Overman is Nietzsche's master, the kind of person who rises above the herd, and goes "beyond" good and evil in creating value out of power, strength and domination.

No.73
To what are you referring?
Oh, I see what you mean now...

 1/ Helicopter view: Gottlob Frege (1848–1925) is widely recognized as ushering in the modern resurgence of formal logic in the West, as well as being the father of *analytic philosophy*, which refers to a school of early 20th-century thinking in Europe and the US that emphasized symbolic logical notation, the philosophy of language, and empiricism as the real "business" and purview of philosophy. He showed that logic is the basis for mathematics, and offered the world the function, which is a relation whereby each acceptable input (called a range) has exactly one output (called the domain), and looks like this: $x \mapsto f(x)$. In the philosophy of language, Frege put forward the *context principle*, whereby one should never "ask for the meaning of a word in isolation, but only in the context of a proposition". This may seem obvious to most people, but philosophers are notorious for picking apart singular terms and defining them. However, we all know that we need to understand the context of any word utilized, and many a literature professor beats this principle into his/her students – and has had this principle beaten into him/her – because of Frege. Frege offered many other significant ideas to the world, but his most famous is the distinction between *sense* and *reference*.

Gottlob Frege // 1848–1925

2/ Shortcut: The *reference* of a word is the relationship between the linguistic expression – say, William Shakespeare – and the entity in the real world to which that linguistic expression refers. The *sense*, or *meaning*, of the word is purely a linguistic thing, and is defined in relation to other words and expressions in the system of language being utilized. So, there could be words that have a sense/meaning, but no reference. *Hamlet* and *Macbeth* have senses, but no references. On the other hand, William Shakespeare has a sense *and* a reference. Furthermore, there could be linguistic expressions that have references, but no senses. The proverbial "rocket scientist" is aware of things (references), and has names for those things (senses), of which the majority of people on the planet are completely unaware – and probably never could become aware even if they tried!

Frege writes that *sense* is something possessed by a name, such as "Hamlet", whether or not it has a *reference* (an entity in the real world to which the name refers).

See also //
20 Knowledge, p.44
74 Who shaves the barber in town?, p.152

MACBETH.

HAMLET

MISS ELLEN TERRY AS "LADY MACBETH."

3/ Hack: *Reference* points to an entity in the real world to which that word is referring, while *sense* is more like the simple meaning of a word, and is defined in relation to other words and expressions in the linguistic system.

No.74
Who shaves the barber in town? Russell's paradox

Bertrand Russell // 1872–1970

1/ Helicopter view: If you've taken a mathematics class, you've probably heard of *set theory* because most mathematical objects (numbers, functions, relations, etc.) are actually defined in terms of sets. Naïve Set Theory (NST) is one type of set theory. One example of an axiom in NST is *membership* (x is a member of set A, x ∈ A, as in, for example, "the barber is a member of the set of people in a small town who don't shave themselves"). Common mathematical sets include real numbers (values along a number line), natural numbers (0, 1, 2, 3, etc.) and integers (numbers without a fractional component), among many others. However, shortly after NST came into existence, English mathematician-philosopher Bertrand Russell (1872–1970) showed a fatal flaw in its basic axiom having to do with membership. Consider the barber mentioned above, the one who is "a member of the set of people in a small town who don't shave themselves". Does the barber shave himself? (For the purposes of simplicity, we will assume here that the barber is male.)

In modern mathematical set theory, the paradox is considered resolved – but only at the expense of additional restrictions on what is permitted.

2/Shortcut: Answering the barber-shaving question results in a paradox in NST, in which an object is defined in terms of a class of objects that contains the object being defined. This results in a logical contradiction. The barber cannot shave himself, as he only shaves those who do not shave themselves. If he did shave himself, then he would no longer be the barber! On the other hand, if the barber does not shave himself, then he is "a member of the set of people in a small town who don't shave themselves," and hence, *qua* barber, must shave himself! This paradox has come to be known as the Barber Paradox; however, the underlying problem of NST's ability to construct the set of all sets that don't contain themselves is known as Russell's Paradox.

See also //

20 Knowledge, p.44

73 To what are you referring?, p.150

3/Hack: The logical contradiction that arises as a result of Naïve Set Theory's ability to construct the set of all sets that don't contain themselves is known as Russell's Paradox.

No.75
William James' pragmatism

In praise of commonsense

1/ Helicopter view: William James (1842–1910) was a philosopher and psychologist who taught at Harvard University in the USA, who produced works such as *The Principles of Psychology* (1890) that bridge the gap between science and philosophy, or rather "consciousness". (*The Principles* is an account of how the brain is related to the mind.)

The approach known as Pragmatism, however, is considered to have originated in around 1870 (still in the USA) in the writings of Charles Sanders Peirce (1839–1914), rather than those of William James. Nonetheless, it was James who popularized the approach and coined the term when he published a series of lectures entitled "Pragmatism: A New Name for an Old Way of Thinking" in 1907. In these, he starts by identifying what he calls the "perpetual dilemma" of philosophy: of having to choose between the insights of science, on the one hand, and those derived from religion and morality on the other.

James "pragmatically" (we might say) searched for a philosophy that was both empiricist in its adherence to facts and yet could still find a role for religious belief.

William James // 1842–1910

However, as he wrote, all that seemed to be on offer to philosophers at the time was "an empirical philosophy that is not religious enough and a religious philosophy that is not empirical enough for your purpose".

For James, Pragmatism was a "mediating philosophy" that would heal the split between the philosophies of the tender-minded and the tough-minded, and overcome philosophy's perpetual dilemma.

2/ Shortcut: James describes what he calls a "clash of human temperaments", distinguishing between "tough-minded" scientists, and their empirically obtained facts, on the one hand, and "tender-minded" spiritualists who are guided both by *a priori* principles that appeal to the intellect and a commitment to search for eternal values on the other. (Note: *A priori* is the term used by Immanuel Kant [1724–1804; see pages 122–5] for statements that can be seen to be true "by reason alone"; that is, just by a consideration of the meaning of the terms used in them.) While the tender-minded believe in "free will", the "tough-minded" are resolutely "fatalistic".

US philosopher John Dewey (1859 –1952) is considered one of the key pragmatist thinkers (below).

See also //

20 Knowledge, p.44

77 Perceiver, perception and perceived, p.158

3/ Hack: Pragmatism is a philosophical approach that seeks to show that science, on the one hand, and morality and religion, on the other, need not always be in opposition.

No.76
Edmund Husserl's phenomenology

An obscure idea with considerable influence

Edmund Husserl // 1859–1938

1/Helicopter view: Edmund Husserl (1859–1938) was born in today's Czech Republic, although he is often remembered as a German philosopher. More importantly, he is credited as the key figure behind the approach known as phenomenology. The term "phenomenology" is, in fact, a little older, going back to at least the 18th century and the Swiss-German mathematician and philosopher Johann Heinrich Lambert (1728–1777), who used it to describe a method for distinguishing truth from illusion and error. Since many philosophers after Husserl have also used the term in different ways, phenomenology has truly become one of philosophy's vaguest ideas.

Nonetheless, we are able to look with confidence at how the term started out in Husserl's writings. Husserl's first observation is that everything known to us is derived from consciousness. Although the objects of consciousness, or phenomena, are originally accessed through one or other of the physical senses, consciousness then recognizes and plays with these phenomena via perception or belief or through thought or desire.

A representation of consciousness by the 17th-century English physician Robert Fludd (above).

2/ Shortcut: Husserl wanted to outline a method for exploring, not phenomena, but human perceptual and evaluative facilities. Although he wished to speak as a scientist, he insisted that it is not necessary for the objects of the mind to exist in the empirical sense as, in reality, the mind only ever deals with its own impressions and representations. What Husserl calls *knowledge-of-things* is limited to these objects of consciousness, even if – as Immanuel Kant (1724–1804; see pages 122–5) had argued earlier – there is another more fundamental layer to reality.

Husserl uses the term "intentionality" to describe the key relationship between the objects of consciousness and the acts of consciousness themselves. He realizes, however, that the "self" itself cannot be another act, but merely the observer of acts. Accordingly, and again following Kant, Husserl sees the perceiving self as "transcendental" and outside the spatio-temporal order. This conclusion was specifically rejected by Martin Heidegger (1889–1976; see pages 162–3), but enthusiastically adopted by French existentialists such as Jean-Paul Sartre (1905–1980; see pages 166–7) and Simone de Beauvoir (1908–1986; see pages 188–9).

Sartre and de Beauvoir meeting Che Guevara in 1960. Sartre wrote that Castro inspired revolutionary consciousness in Cubans while condemning such consciousness when it was used to criticize state authority.

See also //

20 Knowledge, p.44

77 Perceiver, perception and perceived, p.158

79 Martin Heidegger's *Being and Time*, p.162

3/ Hack: Husserl wanted phenomenology to be a science of consciousness, rather than concern itself merely with empirical things.

No.77
Perceiver, perception and perceived
Wittgenstein's beetle in a box

Ludwig Wittgenstein // 1889–1951

1/ Helicopter view: It seems obvious that other people, places and things – even mathematical concepts – exist "out there" beyond our perceptions of them. However, take a moment to think about what you are aware of when you perceive things. There is the *perceiver* (ego, I or mind) who *has* the perceptions; one's *perceptions of* people, places, things, and so on; and the *external objects* of one's perception, the actual people, places, things, and so on, "out there" themselves. But once we make this distinction, then we can see how this kind of question emerges: if there is my world of perceptions and a world outside of me, then how, if at all, can I get beyond these perceptions to know if they match up or correspond with reality? Now we are moving into *idealism* where, if we're not careful, we could become trapped in our own minds. One route out of idealism has been proposed through a common language argument whereby one person notices that another person seems to perceive and name the same things in a similar way. So, Jenny and Jimmy both talk about the fact that they see a furry, four-legged, fluffy creature in front of them that meows and purrs, and they agree to name it "cat". They take their personal experiences and translate them – as it were – into a common language that can be shared to create communication.

The English philosopher A J Ayer disagreed with Wittgenstein's private language argument, saying that we are supplied with a vocabulary for describing our mental life through analogies.

2/ Shortcut: Ludwig Wittgenstein (1889–1951) disagreed with what Jenny and Jimmy were doing. He put forward his *private language argument* utilizing an illustration where we are to imagine everyone having his or her own beetle in a box to which the word "beetle" corresponds. However, no one is ever allowed to look inside anyone else's box; thus, there's no way for some Jenny to verify that what some Johnny is calling a beetle *is in fact* a beetle, and vice versa. Analogously, there is no way to conclude that words like "pain", "green" and "beetle" corresponding in one person's mind to those things are corresponding in exactly the same way in someone else's mind to those things.

See also //

20 Knowledge, p.44

55 George Berkeley's *esse est percipi*, p.114

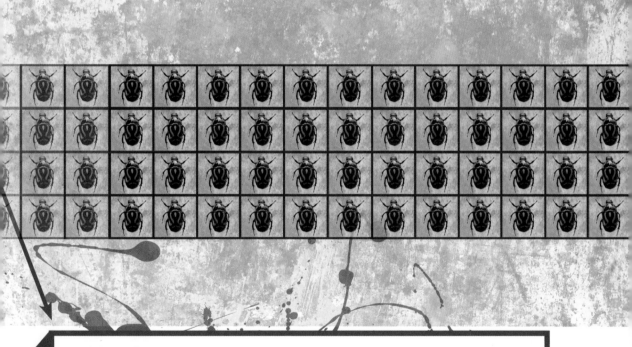

3/ Hack: In the same way that I can imagine you having something in your box that you call a beetle, but I never see it and hence can never be sure if we're really talking about the same thing when we refer to your beetle in your box, so, too, can I never "get inside your head" – so to speak – and know your perspective. Therefore, I can never really know if we're talking about the same things when we're talking about them.

Moritz Schlick's Logical Positivism

Making rules about what to ask

Moritz Schlick // 1838–1916

1/Helicopter view: In 1922, Moritz Schlick (1838–1916), a philosopher-scientist, became Professor of Philosophy at the University of Vienna. Around Schlick gathered the so-called Vienna Circle of very dry, very scientific thinkers, some of whom described themselves as "logical positivists". The Vienna Circle itself was never formally defined, nor yet was Logical Positivism. However, it seems that every member shared a conviction that all claims about the world fall into three categories. First, there are scientific claims that can be checked using practical, empirical procedures of "verification". Second, there are logical and linguistic claims that can be demonstrated simply by a consideration of the meanings of the terms used. Third, all other kinds of statements, including many of the traditional "grand questions" of philosophy – such as "What is the nature of Time?" and "Can we know the nature of the Absolute?" – are dismissed as "unanswerable", which is a nice way of saying that they are "meaningless".

The mathematics faculty and library at the University of Vienna (right), where the Logical Positivists met.

2/ Shortcut: The clearest formulation of Logical Positivism came from Schlick in an article for *The Philosopher* magazine in 1936, entitled simply "Unanswerable Questions". In this he starts by mocking the idea that the final and most important truths are permanently hidden from our eyes or that access to "the key to the Riddle of the Universe" is "barred to all mortals by the very nature of the Universe". He warns that:

See also //
45 Francis Bacon's gift to science, p.94
58 Baron d'Holbach's metaphysical monism, p.120

"According to this common belief, there are many questions which we can formulate, and whose meaning we can grasp completely, though it is definitely impossible to know their answer which is beyond the nature and necessary boundary of all knowledge."

Thus, it will be seen that the Logical Positivists saw their role as advancing human knowledge by removing the distractions and "dead ends", as it were, of poorly constructed and ill-directed enquiries. The fact that this ruled out many of the concerns of aesthetics and ethics, along with many of the perennial debates of mainstream philosophy, was accepted. The new scientific philosophy was limited to checking the logical structure of other people's claims.

3/ Hack: Logical Positivists hold that meaningful questions must be answerable either though practical investigation or by logical and linguistic analysis of their component terms.

No.79
Martin Heidegger's
Being and Time
The inauthentic in search of the authentic

1/ Helicopter view: *Being and Time* by Martin Heidegger (1889–1976) is a much-lauded work of contradictions. This is, first, because it is based on the theories and writings of Edmund Husserl (1859–1938; see pages 156–7), Heidegger's university tutor, to whom the book was originally dedicated. Heidegger later removed the dedication, however, and instead spoke of his work as being built out of the ruins of the destruction of Husserl's views, which he dismissed as "neo-Kantian". Nonetheless, it is unambiguously Husserl's theory that is revisited at great length in *Being and Time*. Second, much of the fame for Heidegger's work comes from its adoption by Marxists, yet Heidegger himself was an enthusiastic member of the German Nazi Party (as were many German academics of the period) and aspired to be the official philosopher of the Nazi movement. It was, in fact, his early association with Husserl that dogged his pursuit of that career, because Husserl was Jewish.

Martin Heidegger // 1889–1976

To make sense of *Being and Time*, however, it must be understood in terms of how Heidegger himself saw it, which is as the philosophical basis for a new politics. Reclaiming language and meaning is at the heart of the project. Heidegger believed that Germany was the true heir to the language and philosophy of Ancient Greece, and that only the two languages of those two states were capable of expressing great thoughts – all the other European languages had been Latinized.

Heidegger wrote that being neo-Kantian is to go "hand in hand with liberalism" and betray "man in his historical enrootedness...."

2/ Shortcut: Where, philosophically speaking, the Greeks had identified the need to resolve the question of *Being*, it was now only the Germans who were capable of continuing the investigation. For Heidegger, the Greek philosopher Plato (428–348 BCE; see pages 40–5) and his book *The Republic* were the most important political reference. Here, an elite and austere political class rules through control of information and steely resolve. Using the term *Volk* to mean a community rooted in a homeland and united by a spiritual purpose, Heidegger writes earnestly:

"All this implies that this *Volk*, as a historical *Volk*, must move itself and thereby the history of the West beyond the centre of their future 'happening' and into the primordial realm of the powers of *Being*."

Hitler at a meeting of the Nazi Party in 1930. He described his aim then in terms of creating a new kind of German consciousness – a task that Heidegger hoped to share.

See also //

76 Edmund Husserl's phenomenology, p.156

80 Existential nihilism, p.164

3/ Hack: Heidegger warns against the technical rationality embodied both in philosophical logic and in the machines of modernity, and urges a return to what he calls "authenticity".

No.80
Existential nihilism
No inherent meaning to life

Friedrich Heinrich Jacobi // 1743–1819

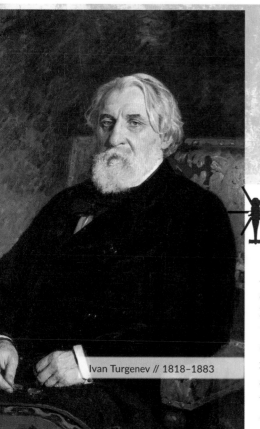

Ivan Turgenev // 1818–1883

1/Helicopter view: The word "nihilism" is derived from the German *Nihilismus*, which itself comes from the Latin *nihil*, with the meaning of "nothing at all". The German philosopher Friedrich Heinrich Jacobi (1743–1819) used the term to mean "the doctrine of negation" with respect to religion or morals, while the Russian author Ivan Turgenev (1818–1883) used *nigilizm* in his novel *Fathers and Sons* (1862), which is revered as one of the major works of 19th-century fiction. There are a few types of nihilism. *Moral nihilism* is what Friedrich Nietzsche (1844–1900; see pages 148–9) had in mind when he claimed that "God is dead", since, from his perspective, the Christian God was no longer a viable source of any moral principles in the West, therefore leading to a rejection of an objective and universal moral law, as well as a sense of moral obligation. *Epistemological nihilism* is a rejection of any universal truths or meanings; there could be relative truths or meanings, however. *Cosmic nihilism* sees nature through scientific eyes as wholly indifferent, valueless and lacking in intelligibility.

In *The Will to Power*, Nietzsche embraces nihilism, saying that it is "not only the belief that everything deserves to perish; but one actually puts one's shoulder to the plough; one destroys".

2/Shortcut: Of the different types of nihilism, *existential nihilism* is probably the most fascinating, and refers to the belief that there is no inherent meaning or purpose to life, the universe, reality or anything in existence. It could be argued that existential nihilism is an effect or a result of the other three nihilisms (moral, epistemological and cosmic); after all, a cold, dark, godless, moral-less, truth-less, value-less, indifferent universe lends itself nicely to a meaningless one as well. The Greek poet Theognis of Megara (6th century BCE) may have summed life up nicely for the existential nihilist: "It is best for man were he never to have been born or to have seen the light of the Sun; but, if once born the next best thing is for him to pass through the gates of death as speedily as he can…"

See also //

70 The Kyoto School and nothingness, p.144

81 Existential authenticity, p.166

3/Hack: Existential nihilism is the belief that there is no inherent meaning of or purpose to life, the universe, reality or anything in existence.

No.81
Existential authenticity
Truth, lucidity and freedom

Simone de Beauvoir // 1908–1986   Jean-Paul Sartre // 1905–1980

1/ Helicopter view: The Greek *authenteó* means "self-doer" or "self-governor", and it is from this that the English word *authenticity* is derived. Authenticity in the philosophical sense denotes something more along the lines of "the original or genuine state of human existence". The concept arises from the insights of existentialists such as Jean-Paul Sartre (1905–1980) and Simone de Beauvoir (1908–1986; see pages 188–9), which suggest that humans live in an inauthentic way because the norms, cultural values and societal laws they construct contribute to a false picture of reality and one's place in it. According to existentialists, experiences such as anxiety, dread and facing your own death, as well as a radical re-examination of habitual lifestyles, cultural contexts and ways of thinking, are important because they reveal basic truths about our own condition as humans. What one begins to see is that becoming authentic is initially a matter of openly and honestly grasping the gravity of one's existence as an individual, namely, the raw fact that "I exist" – thus, the *exist*-ing part of existentialism – and then of creating meaning in one's life, and acting on that meaning.

For many, Edvard Munch's iconic painting *The Scream* (right) expresses Sartre's idea of existential angst.

2/Shortcut: Once a person attains authenticity and realizes their situation, then he or she is truly "free" in a variety of senses: free from the ignorance that is a natural inhibitor of our minds; free from the false constructs that have been erected around us; and free to make meaningful and valuable whatever it is that we deem worthy.

See also //
57 David Hume's compatibilism, p.118
80 Existential nihilism, p.164

3/Hack: According to existentialists, to be authentic is to have a true and lucid consciousness of reality – which entails grasping the raw fact that "I exist", as well as seeing through the false constructs that have been erected around us – and this will lead to a variety of freedoms.

No.82

Karl Popper's falsifiability

Showing a hypothesis to be false

Karl Popper // 1902–1994

1/ Helicopter view: Let's say that you put dog food out for your dog, Rex, every night for him to eat in the morning. You then take him upstairs to sleep in your bed every night, with your bedroom door locked, but come downstairs every morning to discover that his food has been eaten. Now, let's say you generate a couple of hypotheses to explain how the food is being eaten:

Hypothesis 1: Rex unlocks the door, opens it, goes downstairs, eats his food, then comes back upstairs, shuts the door, locks it, then gets back into bed with you.

Hypothesis 2: Houses have cracks and crevices, and there is a mouse (or mice) living behind the wall that comes out every night to eat Rex's food.

Hypothesis 3: There is a Crumpkin, a being that cannot be seen or detected by any instruments, which transports into the house, eats Rex's food, then transports back out.

Hamlet, Horatio, Marcellus and the Ghost (1796) as imagined by Henry Fuseli (right). Regardless of whether there really was a ghost, it had a real effect on Hamlet.

A lot of people would entertain the possibility of Hypothesis 1 occurring, and if you were a dog-trainer by trade, we might take such a hypothesis seriously. Almost every sane person on the planet would rule out Hypothesis 3, however. But why?

2/ Shortcut: One reason is that Hypothesis 3 could never be *shown* to be false, by observation or by experiment, ever. It is simply impossible to do, given the definition of a Crumpkin. There is no test that can be devised to confirm or disconfirm the Crumpkin hypothesis. This is the doctrine of *falsifiability*, according to one of the greatest philosophers of science, Karl Popper (1902–1994), and he used it to distinguish science from pseudoscience and religion.

See also //

45 Francis Bacon's gift to science, p.94

83 Shifting paradigms, p.170

3/ Hack: Falsifiability is the doctrine that for a hypothesis to count, as in the purview of science, it must be able to be shown to be false, by observation or by experiment.

No.83
Shifting paradigms
Revolutionary thinking in science

1/ Helicopter view: When the Greek philosopher Xenophon (*c.*430–350 BCE) claimed the Sun was really just a red-hot stone, the mythologists who had long held that the Sun was the god Helios driving his chariot across the sky on a daily basis probably laughed at him – then wanted him dead, no doubt. So, too, when Nicolaus Copernicus (1473–1543) formulated a model of the universe with the Sun motionless at the centre, and the planets revolving around it rather than the Earth, as had been upheld by theologians and philosophers in the West since the time of Aristotle (384–322 BCE; see pages 46–53), he reluctantly published his ideas with the proviso that the work was more of a mathematical fiction. Why? Well, because otherwise he would have been jailed and possibly executed by the Catholic Church of the time. Many new ideas have emerged in the history of science, medicine and technology that, at first, were completely misunderstood, ignored, laughed at, rejected and/or condemned by the established community. For example, Galileo (1564–1642) fought hard to demonstrate that the natural state of things is motion, and not rest, as had been assumed since at least Aristotle; Sir Isaac Newton (1643–1727) upturned the scientific world with his theory of gravity, as did Robert Hooke (1635–1703) with cell theory, Charles Darwin (1809–1882) with evolution, and Albert Einstein (1879–1955) with relativity.

Thomas Kuhn // 1922–1996

The theory of heavenly spheres as portrayed by the Portuguese cartographer Bartolomeu Velho in 1568 (right). It survived by growing ever more complex regardless of falsifiability.

2/ Shortcut: When a radical shift in scientific thinking takes place, we have what Thomas Kuhn (1922–1996) referred to as a *paradigm shift* – a fundamental change in the foundational world view, thought processes, behaviours and practices of a particular scientific discipline. The "old" science no longer works, and may even die a very long death.

See also //

45 Francis Bacon's gift to science, p.94

82 Karl Popper's falsifiability, p.168

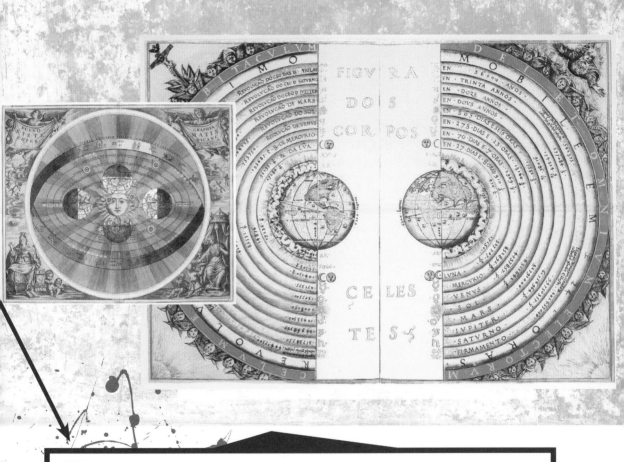

3/ Hack: The concept of paradigms fighting each other to death, as it were, is a valuable antidote to the conventional notion of science as a process of the smooth accumulation of facts.

No.84
Feminist philosophy

Riding the waves

1/Helicopter view: There are many reasons we can give for it – genetics, brain chemistry, personality, social structures, or a combination of all these factors. The fact of the matter is that, in general, no matter what culture we consider on the planet, the history of humanity has always been *androcentric* (the Greek word anēr means "male" or "man"), where the masculine perspective has been the dominant point of view. Masculinity is usually associated with virility, rationality, power, dominance and violence. What this has meant for women, therefore, is a history of always being the "Second Sex" – to quote the mid-20th-century feminist Simone de Beauvoir (1908–1986; see pages 188–9). It gets worse: up until only the last 100 years or so, women were not allowed to attend school, to govern, to vote, to own property or to work in any number of trades. In the West, these male-chauvinist perspectives started to change during the Enlightenment, especially after the publication of *A Vindication of the Rights of Woman* (1792), a work by Mary Wollstonecraft (1759–1797; see pages 136–7) in which she argued that women are capable of reason, but have not been given the opportunity to go to school. By the 1920s, women in parts of the Western world had more access to education and to professions; they had some property rights; they could sue people; and they had the right to vote. New Zealand was actually the first country to sanction women's suffrage. This is known as the *first wave* of feminism.

Emmeline Pankhurst and the Suffragettes campaigned for equal rights through civil disobedience (above). The American wartime propaganda poster "We Can Do It!" (right) has long been used to promote feminism.

2/ Shortcut: The *second wave* of feminism is usually associated with *The Feminine Mystique* (1963), a work by Betty Friedan (1921–2006) in which she argues that sexist oppression is all pervasive and deeply embedded in every area of life. Friedan ends her book by advocating education and meaningful work as the most important methods by which women can avoid becoming trapped in a false consciousness created by feminine stereotypes.

See also //

66 Mary Wollstonecraft's vindication, p.136

92 Simone de Beauvoir's *Second Sex*, p.188

We Can Do It!

POST FEB. 15 TO 1.28 • WAR PRODUCTION CO-ORDINATING COMMITTEE

Betty Friedan // 1921–2006

3/ Hack: Second-wave feminism advocates a radical transformation of almost every aspect of political and personal life, which is unjustly tilted in favour of men and the male perspective.

No.85

Jean-François Lyotard's post-modernism

Jean-François Lyotard // 1930–2004

Out with the old rules!

1/ Helicopter view: Post-modernism is a late 20th-century movement in Western philosophy, characterized by a sceptical approach to truth and values in general, as well as – despite the inherent contradiction – with an overtly political opposition to what is seen as the "ideologies" that lie behind political and economic power. The movement straddles many areas of the arts and knowledge, but within philosophy it is particularly associated with the writings of the French philosopher Jean-François Lyotard (1930–2004) and his 1979 book *La Condition Postmoderne*, which was published five years later in English as *The Postmodern Condition: A Report on Knowledge*. In this, Lyotard adapts elements of an earlier philosophical debate about the workings of natural language to offer a radically different perspective on the "game rules" for science, art and literature.

The post-modernist sees "a strict interlinkage between the kind of language called science and the kind called ethics and politics" and this interlinkage underlies and creates the entire cultural and philosophical perspective of the West. As German philosopher Max Weber (1864–1920) foresaw, science is necessarily interwoven with government and administration, especially in the computer age, where information is the key commodity.

2/Shortcut: Lyotard sees the emphasis in the human search for knowledge as shifting away from the ends of human action to its means, a shift that has led to an increasing separation of science and philosophy. "I define postmodern as incredulity toward meta-narratives," he writes. Knowledge becomes disassociated and compartmentalized, and the end result is a "loss of meaning" itself. However, the true post-modernist does not regret this, but rather suggests that judgement on all issues must ultimately be aesthetic.

Lyotard sees a world in which imagination and reason are in disharmony, but, recalling the words of Immanuel Kant (1724–1804; see pages 122–5) and Edmund Burke (1729–1797), he characterizes this as the world of the sublime. For Lyotard, the post-modern sublime occurs when we are unable to employ reason to understand the grand spectacle of modernity.

The Betrayal of Images: 'Ceci n'est pas une pipe' (1929) by Belgian surrealist artist René Magritte. Magritte explored the relationship of words to the world through visual puns and tricks.

See also //
83 Shifting paradigms, p.170
86 Jacques Derrida's deconstruction, p.176

3/Hack: Post-modernism challenges the expert's claim to knowledge and offers instead a questioning philosophical role: the post-modernist "makes no claims to being original or even true", or suggests that their hypotheses should "be accorded predictive value in relation to reality", but only that their statements should have "strategic value".

No.86
Jacques Derrida's deconstruction
Playing jiggery-pokery with words

1/Helicopter view: The term "deconstruction" was introduced to European philosophy in the 1960s by French philosophy professor Jacques Derrida (1930–2004), but its roots go a little deeper, with a clear debt – as with much modern French philosophy – to the writings of Edmund Husserl (1859–1938; see pages 156–7). Husserl described what he called a "dismantling", and his approach was further developed by one of his students, Martin Heidegger (1889–1976; see pages 162–3), as the "destruction" of theories. The approach is also descended from the attempt to describe the workings of language as a set of signs made by Ferdinand de Saussure (1857–1913).

Derrida's particular development of the notion is to identify a series of what he calls fundamental oppositions. These include:

- Good/Evil
- Past/Future
- Is/Is Not
- Speech/Writing
- Body/Soul
- Transcendent/Empirical
- Culture/Nature

He sees one side of each pair as dominant, and his first aim is to reduce the power of that one. He argues that both approaches have equal explanatory power and that in each case a third term can be found that transcends the opposition. In this respect, deconstruction is again mimicking the dialectic of Georg Wilhelm Friedrich Hegel (1770–1831; see pages 132–3). And like Hegel, Derrida speaks of his new synthesis as superior to what has gone before.

However, there are other texts by Derrida that appear to say something very different; this is also part of the "deconstructionist" approach. Derrida often opposed his own earlier views, and challenged all and any interpretations of them, claiming to do so was part of a deeper philosophical process.

"This interweaving, this textile, is the text produced only in the transformation of another text", says Derrida obscurely in *Semiology and Grammatology*.

2/ Shortcut: Derrida grandly claims that all the other thinkers' and philosophers' ideas, theories and conclusions can be dismissed as merely the products of an elaborate word game that they have been playing. However, what he puts in their place also looks like a word game. He says that deconstruction is concerned with the "wholly other", and that he wishes to overthrow the "metaphysics of presence", which he describes as the valuing of truth as "self-identical immediacy" sustained by the "ontological priority" of speech over writing. And all of this, he says, is rooted in the violent exclusion of "otherness".

See also //

83 Shifting paradigms, p.170

85 Jean-François Lyotard's postmodernism, p.174

Jacques Derrida // 1930–2004

3/ Hack: Deconstruction is a mix, some would say a hodgepodge, of ideas from earlier philosophers, which not only make no sense, but are supposed to make no sense – because part of the theory is that meaning must be "deconstructed" – or destroyed.

Alvin Plantinga // b.1932

Alvin Plantinga's basic beliefs

What would God do?

1/ Helicopter view: Alvin Plantinga is a 20th-century American philosopher (b.1932) who has attempted to employ the techniques of modern logic to investigate classical questions concerning belief in God. His starting point is that there is a parallel between belief in the existence of God and belief in the existence of other minds. The question of how we can know, for example, that other people think like us, rather than being merely collections of automated responses in the manner of robots or automata, goes back to Ancient times and was expressed by René Descartes (1596–1650; see pages 102–7) as one of his sceptical doubts.

However, it is another problem – that of why an all-powerful deity would allow evil to exist – to which Plantinga is considered to have given the most insightful response. The Ancient Greek philosopher Epicurus (341–270 BCE; see pages 54–5), for example, reasoned:

"Either God wants to abolish evil, and cannot; or he can, but does not want to. If he wants to, but cannot, he is impotent. If he can, but does not want to, he is wicked. If God can abolish evil, and God really wants to do it, why is there evil in the world?"

This looks like a logical contradiction, but Plantinga argues that it is *only* if people have the opportunity to choose evil over good that they can truly be said to have chosen *not* to commit evil.

The Garden of Earthly Delights (right) is an oil painting in three parts by the Dutch artist Hieronymus Bosch, c.1500. Opinion is divided over the message of the painting.

2/Shortcut: God is logically bound to allow people to choose evil in order to have the greater good, which is people choosing to do good. If this seems like a restriction of God's powers, Plantinga supposes that it is only in the same way that God chooses not to have "round squares", or to allow other logical inconsistencies.

Plantinga's argument has been welcomed by Christian theologians, but others have felt that it does not truly remove the question of why, for example, an all-powerful God could not create people who freely choose not to commit evil. Such a possibility is explicitly discussed by St Augustine of Hippo (354–430 CE; see page 65).

See also //

20 Knowledge, p.44
36 The greatest being conceivable, p.76

3/Hack: Plantinga believes that a world containing creatures who are both able and willing to choose good over evil is better than a world in which that choice has been removed.

John Rawls // 1921–2002

John Rawls' original position

Making moral decisions behind a veil of ignorance

1/ Helicopter view: We want to be able to live peaceful lives as we pursue our needs and wants, free from as much pain as possible, and for the most part we need each other in order to accomplish this. It takes a very special person to live alone, self-sufficient on an island. So what do we do? We form groups in which we interact with one another. Thomas Hobbes (1588–1679; see pages 96–7) suggested we make a social contract with one another, agreeing to live peacefully, because the alternative "state of nature" is a dog-eat-dog world (at times, literally). However, certain members of the group will act in selfish, reprehensible and unjust ways – even after clearly established social norms, rules and laws have been established. Even the people who have agreed to the social contract might be biased in favour of one group or another, or one belief or another, and may set up social conditions that are unfair for certain members of the society. How can we avoid something like this? John Rawls (1921–2002) suggested a thought experiment that legislators might entertain before writing policies, where they envision themselves behind what he called a veil of ignorance. Behind the *veil of ignorance*, one is to consider a new society with new laws where money, position in life, gender and race are not to be considered at all.

The concept of the veil of ignorance (right) has a long pedigree and appears in the thinking of many other philosophers, including John Stuart Mill and Immanuel Kant.

2/Shortcut: Being in a truly equal society, behind a veil of ignorance, is to be in what John Rawls called the *original position*. Each member of society is to be guaranteed all of the basic rights and privileges, since no one is better than anyone else. Also, given that you are not sure if you're going to be a poor person or not in this society once it is up and running, according to Rawls you would also want a system that maximizes the means of those who have the least.

See also //

19 The Republic, p.42
60 Immanuel Kant's moral theory, p.124
68 Good for the majority, p.140

 3/Hack: In the original position, everyone is guaranteed all of the basic rights and privileges in a society, because the policy makers are behind a veil of ignorance.

No.89
Jürgen Habermas' communicative reason
In search of understanding

1/ Helicopter view: The 20th-century German philosopher Jürgen Habermas (b.1929) wrote vociferously over five decades. His early work was sociological in flavour, analyzing the public sphere and modernization, and included critiques of trends in philosophy and politics. This then developed into more theoretical writing concerning rationality, meaning and truth. His two-volume *Theory of Communicative Action* (1981) attempted to systematize these ideas.

Habermas argued that the moral catastrophe of the Second World War need not end hopes for a better world through technology and modernity.

2/Shortcut: Habermas is said to belong to the second generation of Frankfurt School Critical Theorists. Like much of the school's work, his writing is obscure and heavily jargonized. However, the contrast between the early and late Frankfurt School shown here concerns those who drew a picture of Enlightenment rationality inherently wedded to domination and those, like Habermas, who defended it as an "unfinished" emancipatory project. Habermas says that the moral catastrophe of the Second World War need not lead to a rejection of hopes for increasing rationality and human emancipation through technology and modernity.

See also //
60 Immanuel Kant's moral theory, p.124
68 Good for the majority, p.140
88 John Rawls' original position, p.180

For Habermas, the danger for humanity instead comes from conflating a narrow kind of instrumental rationality with rationality itself – mistaking technical control for the entirety of communication. Building on the writings of his fellow countryman Max Weber (1864–1920), who described the various kinds of rationality that he considered made up the structures of society, Habermas offers an account of what he calls "communicative rationality". This is centred on a quest for mutual understanding rather than the achievement of certain aims or aspirations, or as part of a search for authenticity. Part of this is what Habermas calls the "paradoxical achievement of intersubjectivity". Here, "intersubjectivity" relates to communication between two separate, conscious minds. The paradox is that in order to communicate, two people must both assume the other person is like him/herself and at the same time acknowledge that there are important differences. One example that has been offered as a means of understanding this concept is that of a pilot and a co-pilot engaged in the very particular conversation necessary to jointly fly an aeroplane.

Jürgen Habermas // b.1929

3/Hack: "Communicative rationality" locates rationality in the structures of linguistic communication, as discussed by others such as the English philosopher J L Austin (1911–1960) and the American John Searle (b.1932). It is based on the idea that all speech acts share an inherent purpose: the goal of mutual understanding.

No.90
Edmund Gettier's Gettier Problem Searching for certainty

1/ Helicopter view: The Gettier Problem is actually an ancient debate presented by Plato (428–348 BCE; see pages 40–5) in his dialogue *Theaetetus* (see page 45). However, it is often, if erroneously, credited to the 20th-century American professor Edmund Gettier (b.1927), who revisited it from a new and rigorously logical standpoint. Both Plato and Gettier start by considering the conditions necessary for a statement to count as true. These are:

Condition 1: You believe something to be true.

Condition 2: You have good, relevant reasons for your belief (it is "justified").

Condition 3: And your belief is "true"; the world is as you think.

However, in certain circumstances, all three of these conditions may be satisfied and yet we might feel that someone should not really be said to "know something".

A farmer thinks he can see his cow in the field, and it is indeed there. Yet, can the farmer be said to know it?

2/Shortcut: Gettier offers as thought experiments some clumsy counterexamples concerning the beliefs of two men with coins in their pockets. The American philosopher Roderick Chisholm (1916–1999) later responded with a slightly better one concerning an

See also //
20 Knowledge, p.44
56 Not all swans are white, p.116

animal that appears to be an animal but isn't, while in 1999, I myself came up with a much-quoted example of "the cow in the field". As this is a lot clearer, I will give it again here:

Suppose that a farmer wants to check up on whether his cow, Daisy, is safely grazing in a field. He goes to the field and sees a black and white shape in the distance that looks like his cow. He concludes it is his cow and that she is safely grazing in his field. However, unknown to him, what he sees is merely a large piece of paper caught in a bush. On the other hand, Daisy is in the field, but out of sight, grazing in a hollow.

The key point here, as with the so-called Gettier counterexamples, is that all three conditions for knowledge are met – yet we would hesitate to say that the farmer really "knew" his cow was safe in the field. One response by logicians has been to say that nothing derived from a false belief counts as knowledge. But this seems to be tautological and unhelpful.

3/Hack: The Gettier Problem is concerned with the criteria for something we believe to actually count as "knowledge".

No.91
Richard Dawkins' blind watchmaker A long time coming

1/ Helicopter view: The universe is an amazingly complex thing, that's for sure – and it is made up of things that are amazingly complex themselves too. Take the human eye, for example. Each part – the lens, pupil, cornea, macula, fovea, retina, iris, and so on – has a function that contributes to the overall goal of enabling sight. Now consider that the eye is part of a greater visual system in humans, which itself is only one of many systems in the human body working together to maintain one's existence for a time on the planet. One cannot help but think, then, that there must have been (or still is) some kind of thinking, reasoning, designing being that has "put it all together", so a human can function in the way that it does. The Watchmaker Analogy has been made famous by William Paley (1743–1805; see pages 126–7) in his 1802 book *Natural Theology*, where he argued that the hierarchical complexity and purposiveness of organisms must have a Designer God behind their workings analogous to a watch having an intelligent watchmaker.

Complex organs, like the human eye, seem to be made of parts that only serve a useful purpose when they are assembled together.

2/ Shortcut: Championing evolutionary theory and the idea that there is no longer a need for a Designer God to explain the natural workings of the universe, Richard Dawkins (b.1941) has argued for what he refers to as the *blind watchmaker*, which is his argument that natural selection can explain the complex adaptations of organisms. Over time, with only minor modifications, something like the human eye can emerge from a simple patch of light-sensitive organic material.

See also //

39 The Uncaused Cause, p.82

61 William Paley's watchmaker analogy, p.126

Richard Dawkins // b.1941

3/ Hack: Richard Dawkins argues for the blind watchmaker, the idea that natural selection can explain the complex adaptations of organisms, and that there is no need to posit a watchmaker god.

Simone de Beauvoir's *Second Sex*

Thinking about the Other

Simone de Beauvoir // 1908–1986

1/ Helicopter view: Simone de Beauvoir (1908–1986) is today recognized as one of the most original of the French existentialist philosophers. Working alongside figures such as Jean-Paul Sartre (1905–1980; see pages 166–7), Albert Camus (1913–1960) and Maurice Merleau-Ponty (1908–1961), de Beauvoir not only produced a distinctive corpus of writings, but also played a key role in shaping French existentialism.

De Beauvoir's philosophical approach is notably diverse, with influences including ancient Eastern philosophy (which discusses a very particular kind of consciousness), the German philosophers Georg Wilhelm Friedrich Hegel (1770–1831; see pages 132–3) and Edmund Husserl (1859–1938; see pages 156–7) and also a clutch of French philosophers, from René Descartes (1596–1650; see pages 102–7) to Henri Bergson (1859–1941).

De Beauvoir's first manuscript was, indeed, a work of conventional philosophy, but it was so poorly received by publishers that she shifted toward writing literature – which was something considered more "appropriate" for a woman by the crusty French publishing establishment. Years later, in *The Second Sex* (1949), she attacks the passive role assigned to women by society and the fact that throughout history they have been relegated to a sphere of "immanence". This is a Catholic term that she borrows to mean something like "a state of dwelling within and not extending beyond a given domain".

The very concept of "woman", de Beauvoir argues, is a male concept: woman is always "other" because the male is the "seer": he is the subject and she the object.

2/Shortcut: Although de Beauvoir's novel *The Mandarins* received the prestigious *Prix Goncourt* award in 1954, her most famous and influential work is indubitably *The Second Sex*, which heralded the post-war feminist revolution. Here, de Beauvoir's central theme is that the relationship of men and women is inherently unequal, with women being relegated to the role of being the "Other". Modifying Hegel, she says that there is a general need for the psychological Self to use "otherness" in order to find and define itself, to constitute itself as a subject. However, in human societies, de Beauvoir complains, it is only men who take on the role of the Self. As she explains in her introduction: woman "is the incidental, the inessential, as opposed to the essential. He is the Subject, he is the Absolute – she is the Other."

See also //

66 Mary Wollstonecraft's vindication, p.136

84 Feminist philosophy, p.172

3/Hack: Although *The Second Sex* is on the surface a political call for women to be given higher status, as in all de Beauvoir's works, the themes of freedom, responsibility and ambiguity add a deeper philosophical dimension.

No.93
Hannah Arendt's Banality of Evil

Normalizing horrendous human wickedness

Hannah Arendt // 1906–1975

1/ Helicopter view: Commonsensically, we can describe evil as a state of affairs that results in physical or psychological pain, suffering, distress, destruction, corruption and/or deterioration of some kind. Thinkers have made a distinction between *natural* or *physical* evil and *moral* or *human-made* evil. Consider all the humans and other beings capable of suffering, who lose life and limb as a result of disease, a prenatal condition, genetic disposition, tornadoes, hurricanes, earthquakes, tsunamis or simply by "being in the wrong place at the wrong time" during a natural disaster. We regard the misfortunes that befall them as an evil that stems from the world's natural physical, chemical and/or biological processes. Now consider the school bully who seeks out, humiliates and punches the weak kid in the class; the scammer who takes what is left of grandma's life savings; the thieves that steal the single mother's car from her driveway overnight during the working week; the gang member who feels dissed by a rival thug and shoots him dead in front of the convenience store – all of these are examples of moral evil.

The views of Hannah Arendt (above) have often been co-opted by politicians, particularly in Israel. In fact, from 1944 onward, she characterized mainstream Zionism as reactionary, blood-and-soil nationalism.

2/Shortcut: *Eichmann in Jerusalem: A Report on the Banality of Evil* (1963) is a book by German-born American Hannah Arendt (1906–1975) in which she argues that Adolf Eichmann – one of the orchestrators of The Holocaust – exhibited a new kind of evil, one where such horrendous human wickedness is normalized and seen as an everyday kind of thing. Eichmann was "terribly and terrifyingly normal" – trite, boring and banal in his acceptance of the actions of the Third Reich, a regime that unjustly took the lives of some 21 million people between 1933 and 1945 as a result of genocide, the execution of civilians and prisoners of war, forced labour, the bombing of civilian populations, imposed famine and the resulting diseases, and euthanasia.

The Nuremberg Trials (below), held after the Second World War from 1945–6, were the first international war crimes trials.

See also //

30 Picture perfect?, p.64
72 Friedrich Nietzsche's Overman, p.148

3/Hack: The banality of evil is one where horrendous human wickedness is normalized and seen as an everyday kind of thing.

No.94

Philippa Foot // 1920–2010

Philippa Foot's Trolley Problem

What do you do when all options look bad?

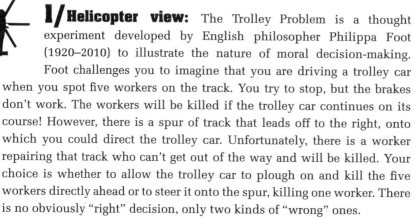

1/ Helicopter view: The Trolley Problem is a thought experiment developed by English philosopher Philippa Foot (1920–2010) to illustrate the nature of moral decision-making.

Foot challenges you to imagine that you are driving a trolley car when you spot five workers on the track. You try to stop, but the brakes don't work. The workers will be killed if the trolley car continues on its course! However, there is a spur of track that leads off to the right, onto which you could direct the trolley car. Unfortunately, there is a worker repairing that track who can't get out of the way and will be killed. Your choice is whether to allow the trolley car to plough on and kill the five workers directly ahead or to steer it onto the spur, killing one worker. There is no obviously "right" decision, only two kinds of "wrong" ones.

You might justify redirecting the trolley car onto the spur, believing that killing one person is "morally better" than killing five. This is the "utilitarian" choice: an act's morality depends on its consequences. The alternative approach is the "deontological", or "principled", one that sees an act as itself moral or immoral, irrespective of the consequences.

Imagine that you are driving a trolley car when you spot five workers on the track ahead – yet the only alternative route is also blocked, if only by one person. Thought experiments like this are used to explore ethical decision-making.

2/ Shortcut: The Trolley Problem has real-world applications. For example, it arises today with autonomous cars, which are programmed for "what-if" decisions. So, here's another quandary: an autonomous car sees two pedestrians step out from behind a bus. The car "realizes" that continuing on its course will kill the two people. But its only other option, to veer onto the pavement, will surely kill one pedestrian. How ought the engineers program the car to behave in such situations? And should their algorithms favour saving the lives of the car's occupants as opposed to those of people outside?

In such scenarios, there's no escaping what ethicists call "intentionality". However, decisions to "do nothing" seem less morally culpable than acting. Researchers have found, for example, that hardly anyone would be prepared to shove another person in front of a runaway truck in order to save several lives a moment later!

See also //

60 Immanuel Kant's moral theory, p.124

68 Good for the majority, p.140

95 Judith Jarvis Thomson's violinist, p.194

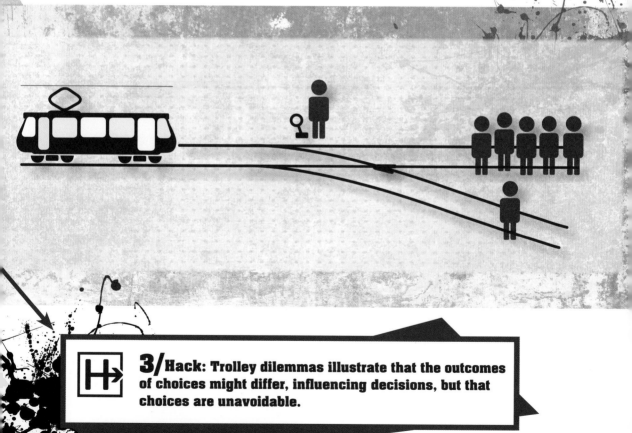

3/ Hack: Trolley dilemmas illustrate that the outcomes of choices might differ, influencing decisions, but that choices are unavoidable.

No.95
Judith Jarvis Thomson's
violinist Machinations by the society of music lovers

1/ Helicopter view: Judith Jarvis Thomson (b.1929) is a 20th-century American moral philosopher who is known for her use of thought experiments to make ethical points. In a much-discussed 1971 journal essay called "A Defense of Abortion", she includes an imaginary scenario intended to show that the right to control your own body should take priority over any obligations to sustain the well-being, or even lives, of others.

Jarvis Thomson asks us to imagine a woman who wakes up one morning to discover that she has been kidnapped by members of a music society and that her body is being used as a life-support machine for a famous violinist. She describes the woman demanding to be "set free", but being urged by doctors to put the interests of the other patient before her own.

For utilitarians, the pleasure the violinist in the thought experiment can give outweighs the interests of the woman kidnapped.

See also //
60 Immanuel Kant's moral theory, p.124
68 Good for the majority, p.140
94 Philippa Foot's Trolley Problem, p.192

2/ Shortcut: There are many alternative versions of the violinist story. One variable is that the human being to be saved need not be "a famous violinist", but an opportunist or criminal instead. Another is that the original patient, "the victim", may find themselves in their difficult situation not as a result of kidnapping or accident, but because of their own carelessness. Jarvis Thomson also considers the possibility that the violinist needs to be connected up, not for nine months, but for as long as the violinist is alive.

Another 20th-century philosopher and ethicist, Philippa Foot (1920–2010; see pages 192–3), starts from a Catholic standpoint and argues that non-provision of a service – in this case, refusing to be connected up as a life-support machine – is different from active harm. In her book *Moral Dilemmas* (2002), Foot argues that the case of abortion is one of committing active harm. However, another English moral philosopher, Brenda Almond (b.1937), stresses that pressure from outsiders on the woman to save the worthy violinist is unreasonable and undeserved in all these cases. She may generously agree to support the life that is dependent on her, but she has no obligation to do so.

Judith Jarvis Thomson // b.1929

3/ Hack: Jarvis Thomson's argument is that being forced to carry a foetus to term is a violation of a woman's right to control her own body.

No.96
Peter Singer's expanding circle

Whose view counts?

Peter Singer // b.1946

1/ Helicopter view: Peter Singer (b.1946) is an Australian moral philosopher who has attempted to reorient ethics away from meta-ethics and toward practical issues such as ecological duties and animal rights. He offers utilitarian arguments that promote the interests of animals and the biosphere, and rejects what he calls "species prejudice" in favour of humans. In this way, the circle of beings and interests considered before arriving at a morally correct policy "expands". On the other hand, because he considers that certain human conditions, such as severe lifelong disability, result in a negative measure of happiness, he has also been accused of excluding some humans from the "expanded circle". Protesters have even linked him to Nazi-era policies of eugenics and disrupted his lectures on visits to Europe.

Peter Singer's two best-known works, written in a clear and accessible style, are *Practical Ethics* (1979) and *Animal Liberation* (1975). A third work, *The Expanding Circle: Ethics, Evolution, and Moral Progress* (1981), essentially offers a systemization of the views expressed in these earlier works.

Peter Singer does not claim that the interests of animals count as equal to those of humans in calculations, but he insists that they do count.

2/Shortcut: Singer's starting point is anthropological, asking "What is ethics?" and "Where do moral rules come from?" Are they based on emotions, reason or some innate sense of right and wrong? Singer argues that although altruism began as a genetically based drive to protect one's kin and community members, which offered a survival advantage to species, it has since developed into a consciously chosen ethic with an expanding circle of moral concern. On the other hand, commenting in 1999 on the reception to his ideas, Singer admitted to having been ultimately frustrated and disappointed. Interviewed by *The New Yorker* magazine about his book *Animal Liberation* in particular, he said, "All you have to do is walk around the corner to McDonald's to see how successful I have been."

See also //

60 Immanuel Kant's moral theory, p.124

68 Good for the majority, p.140

3/Hack: Singer sees the only true measure of right and wrong as the maximization of happiness and the minimization of suffering. As animals can suffer, this implies a massive shift of ethical consideration away from humans and toward the interests of the rest of nature.

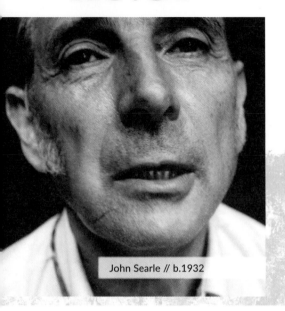

John Searle // b.1932

John Searle's Chinese Room Argument

Taking the measure of artifical intelligence

1/ Helicopter view: John Searle (b.1932) is an American philosopher who presented the "Chinese Room Argument" in 1980 as a contribution to new debates concerning artificial intelligence.

His thought experiment attempts to demonstrate that computers cannot be said to be intelligent just because they may appear to be so. It was a direct response to an earlier challenge by the Second World War code breaker Alan Turing (1912–1954). As a test for intelligence, Turing had proposed the simple method of considering whether someone would be able, given a substantial opportunity to ask questions, to work out whether they were talking to a machine or to another human being. Turing's assertion was that if they cannot, then they ought to consider such a machine to have intelligence.

In Searle's thought experiment, he imagines himself locked in a room with a large pile of Chinese hieroglyphs while someone outside the room posts questions in Chinese through the letterbox for him to sort out. Of course, in the normal way, he could not answer, but what, he says, if inside the room there were some instructions taped on the wall, written in English, which explain precisely which hieroglyph to post back? Then, as Searle puts it, "from the point of view of somebody outside the room in which I am locked, my answers to the questions are absolutely indistinguishable from those of native Chinese speakers".

Alan Turing, aged 16 (above). It was Turing's position concerning artificial intelligence (right) that Searle intended to challenge.

2/Shortcut: The Chinese Room Argument thought experiment is fairly convincing at demonstrating that the person in the room does not understand Chinese. However, one objection often made is that it is not so much the person in the room that appears to understand Chinese, but rather it is the whole "system" – the person in the room, the sets of symbols on the cards, and the instructions taped to the wall – that gives the appearance of understanding. And this is much more plausible. After all, whoever wrote the instructions did really understand Chinese – it took intelligence to write the instructions.

See also //

50 René Descartes' *Cogito*, p.104

51 René Descartes' substance dualism, p.106

98 David Chalmers' philosophical zombies, p.200

3/Hack: Searle's aim is to prove that such a person in such a room does not understand Chinese. And since computers operate in an analogous way, he concludes that it's not really accurate to say that they understand things, even if they produce intelligent-looking responses.

No.98
David Chalmers'
philosophical zombies
Logical possibilities generating metaphysical conclusions

1/ Helicopter view: According to a materialist or physicalist, reality is made up of wholly material/physical things and nothing more. This rules out gods, ghosts and anything supernatural, for certain. But for the hardcore physicalist it also rules out psychological states such as perceptions, beliefs, ideas and other parts of what we call conscious experience. However, most people on the planet think that psychological states are real things of *some* kind, existing in their own right in some way. Australian philosopher David Chalmers (b.1966), and other philosophers of the mind, have put forward arguments for psychological states existing. Such dualistic arguments all have in common the notion that conscious experience cannot be reduced to a physiological process. Chalmers offers a clever argument for dualism, called the zombie argument, where we are supposed to imagine a being that looks and even talks like a human. It goes through all the normal actions and reactions of a human and yet has no psychological states – no consciousness. Now imagine that you have *no idea that it is not like you or me.* Now, if this zombie is logically conceivable – which it is – then this possibility supports an alternative view that sees the world consisting of not just the *physical*, but also the *mental*.

The zombie argument is useful because it brings into focus philosophical debates about consciousness.

2/Shortcut: David Chalmers' argument can be paraphrased like this:

Premise 1: Physicalism says that everything in our world is physical.

Premise 2: If physicalism is true, then a possible metaphysical world must contain everything that our regular physical world contains, including consciousness.

Premise 3: But we can conceive of a zombie world that is exactly like our world physically except that all the zombies lack consciousness.

Conclusion: Physicalism is false.

See also //

50 René Descartes' *Cogito*, p.104

51 René Descartes' substance dualism, p.106

97 John Searle's Chinese Room Argument, p.198

3/Hack: We can conceive of a zombie world that is exactly like our world physically except that all the zombies lack consciousness. Since we can do that, a possible metaphysical world must contain everything that our regular physical world contains, including consciousness.

No.99
Robert Nozick's Pleasure Machine Will it really satisfy your every desire?

1/Helicopter view: The Pleasure Machine, or "Experience Machine", as it is more usually described, is a thought experiment put forward by the American philosopher Robert Nozick (b.1938) in his 1974 book *Anarchy, State, and Utopia.* The point of the experiment is to explore – and indeed challenge – the idea that the only important thing in life is the pursuit of pleasure (an approach that philosophers call "hedonism"). The assumption that pleasure is the decisive good is also at the heart of utilitarianism (see pages 140–1), the theory that judges actions to be right or wrong according to whether they increase or decrease the total amount of happiness in the world.

Nozick describes a machine that is able to provide any user with whatever desirable or pleasurable experiences they want. What is more, the experiences are so realistic that the user cannot distinguish the made-up world from real life. Indeed, the only clue might come (while using the machine) from reflecting that everything was so perfect. But Nozick suggests that one aspect of using the machine is that it is so convincing, you don't even realize you're in it.

Many of the issues raised by Nozick's imaginary machine have begun to be a part of everyday life, as experienced via the internet.

2/Shortcut: Nozick asks, "Would you plug in? What else can matter to us, other than how our lives feel from the inside?"

However, he is sure himself that we would not "plug in" because we put a value on reality, for better or for worse. He concludes: "We learn that something matters to us in addition to experience by imagining an experience machine and then realizing that we would not use it."

Nozick thinks that people are prepared to – at the very least – make some compromises on personal happiness in pursuit of other values. Significantly, Nozick only judges the question in terms of the interests of one individual. However, one might, of course, find a value in the promotion of the happiness of others.

See also //

23 Aristotle's happiness, p.50

25 Epicureanism and Stoicism, p.54

3/Hack: Nozick's aim with his imaginary "Experience Machine" is to show that there are other things than pleasure that have value and increase our well-being.

No.100
The prisoner's dilemma
Should have kept your mouth shut

 1/Helicopter view: The RAND Corporation ("Research ANd Development") was created in 1948 by Douglas Aircraft Company as a think-tank organization for the US Armed Forces. In 1950, at the start of the Cold War and the nuclear arms race, two RAND researchers, Merrill Flood and Melvin Dresher, were devising numerous mathematical models of conflict and co-operation between intelligent, rational decision-makers and, in the midst of their work in game theory, they devised what was subsequently labelled by mathematician Albert Tucker as the *prisoner's dilemma*. The set-up goes something like this: Frank and John are arrested for committing a crime together; the police have insufficient evidence to convict them; they are interrogated separately; and they are told:

The prisoner's dilemma illustrates the parts that communication and the control of information play in arriving at a decision.

John \ Frank	Stays silent:	Testifies against John:
Stays silent:	1. Each serves 2 years	2. John serves 5 years
Testifies against Frank:	3. Frank serves 5 years	4. Each serves 3 years

2/ Shortcut: Now, here's the dilemma. If you were Frank or John, what would you do? What actually happens is that each guy never trusts that the other will keep his mouth shut (Option 4) and that, coupled with the allure of going free (Options 2 and 3), makes it such that each guy ends up testifying against the other (Option 4). They both then serve three years in prison, when the most rational, optimal course of action would have been to keep their mouths shut (Option 1), so that they only had to serve two years. This thought experiment is supposed to show why two completely rational individuals might not co-operate, even if it appears that it would be in their best interests to do so.

See also //
20 Knowledge, p.44
47 Pascal's Wager, p.98

3/ Hack: The prisoner's dilemma is meant to show why two completely rational individuals might not co-operate, even if it appears that it would be in their best interests to do so.

Index

Acknowledgments
Authors' acknowledgments

I would like to acknowledge Susan, Zoe and Lexi, who have given me clever ways to understand and remember the most important theories.
Robert Arp

I'd like to thank Mark Gottlieb at Trident Media for "guiding the book into port". And a special shout-out to Keith Tidman for detailed ideas and advice on several of the hacks.
Martin Cohen

Both authors would like to thank the team at Octopus.

Picture/artwork credits